Nuffield
Home Economics
NUTRITION

General editor, Nuffield Home Economics
Marie Edwards

Editors of this book
Barbara Lake
Robin Osner

Authors of this book
Frances Brown
Derek Fry
Frank Hogarth
Rosalind Howlett
Barbara Lake
Christine Metcalf
Ann Miller
Robin Osner
Linda Roberts
Janet Thorn
Irene Tilley
Erica Wheeler

Contributors to the Background reading
Lesley Buckley
Frank Curtis
Karen Gunner
Issy Cole-Hamilton
Kate Norbury
Jeremy Shoham

Organizers, Nuffield Home Economics 1977—81
Harry Faulkner
Sharon M. Mansell

The Nuffield-Chelsea Curriculum Trust would also like to thank
the following for their help:

Maureen Blackmore
British Gas
Beta Schofield

Nuffield Home Economics

NUTRITION

Published for the Nuffield-Chelsea Curriculum Trust by Hutchinson Education

Hutchinson & Co. (Publishers) Ltd
An imprint of the Hutchinson Publishing Group
17—21 Conway Street, London W1P 6JD

Hutchinson Group (Australia) Pty Ltd
16—22 Church Street, Hawthorn, Melbourne, Victoria 3122

Hutchinson Group (NZ) Ltd
32—34 View Road, PO Box 40—086, Glenfield, Auckland 10

Hutchinson Group (SA) (Pty) Ltd
PO Box 337, Bergvlei 2012, South Africa

First published 1985

© Nuffield-Chelsea Curriculum Trust 1985

British Library Cataloguing in Publication Data
Nuffield-Chelsea Curriculum Trust
   Nutrition — (Nuffield home economics)
   Pupils' text
   1. Nutrition
   I. Title II. Series
   613.2   TX354

ISBN 0 09 152911 5

Design and art direction by Ivan Dodd

Printed and bound in Great Britain by
Anchor Brendon Ltd, Tiptree, Essex

CONTENTS

Acknowledgements

Ashe Laboratories Ltd: 8.10, 8.14.
BBC Hulton Picture Library: 7.14, 15.7.
Barnaby's Picture Library: 1.1d, 2.9c, 5.1c, 5.9, 6.6a, 8.8b, 8.8d, 10.1, 10.6a, 11.8.
Birds Eye Wall's Ltd: 1.1e, 1.5a, 1.5b, 1.5c.
Professor C.C. Booth, Royal Postgraduate Medical School, Hammersmith Hospital: 4.10.
Bovril Ltd: 3.8.
Dr Brian Bracegirdle: 2.7a, 2.7b.
Bob Bray: 1.3a, 1.3b, 5.1b, 5.11, 5.13, 5.14.
Butter Information Council: 1.5d.
Cadbury Typhoo Ltd: 12.7.
J. Allan Cash Photolibrary: 4.3, 6.5a, 7.2, 7.12, 13.4.
Chelsea College Audio Visual Service Unit: 7.10, 8.1a, 8.1b, 8.3, 9.1, 10.2, 10.6b, 10.6c, 10.10, 12.14, 13.1.
Issy Cole-Hamilton: 11.13.
R.J. Corbin: 6.5c.
A. Cozzi: 14.8.
Farmer's Weekly: 1.1a, 1.1b, 2.9a, 2.9b, 4.4, 5.16a, 5.16b, 5.16c, 6.5b, 12.6.
Food for Thought Restaurant: 14.10.
Food Research Institute: 15.14.
Format Photographers/Brenda Prince: 7.1.
Format Photographers/Maggie Murray: 14.3.
Format Photographers/Joanne O'Brian: 7.11.
Gardner Merchant Ltd: 1.1c.
Sally and Richard Greenhill: 8.8a, 9.9b, 9.15, 10.9, 10.13b, 10.14, 10.15, 11.9, 11.10, 11.11, 12.5b, 12.8, 13.5, 13.11, 14.1, 15.1.
Health Education Council: 5.15.
H.J. Heinz Co. Ltd: 14.7.
Here's Health: 9.8a.
Jim Hopwood: 4.13.
Kingsway Public Relations: 14.4, 14.5.
Nina Konrad: 7.8.
E.D. Lacey: 5.1a, 5.8.
The Mansell Collection: 8.8f, 10.13a.
Ministry of Agriculture, Fisheries, and Food: 8.8e.
Ministry of Agriculture — National Food Survey: 1.7.
Reproduced by courtesy of the Trustees, The National Gallery, London: 8.7a.
Simon Norton: 14.2.

OXFAM: 12.5a, 15.5.
Pasta Information Centre: 9.8b.
Photothon: 6.10.
Michael Plomer: 7.3.
Eileen Preston: 10.11.
Rex Features: 7.6, 8.15, 9.9a, 13.3, 15.4, 15.6.
Chris Richardson: 1.9.
Rowntree Mackintosh plc: 7.13.
Royal College of Physicians, Edinburgh: 12.16.
J. Sainsbury plc: 1.1f, 2.3.
St Bartholomew's Hospital — Department of Medical Illustration: 11.4.
Scottish Tourist Board: 11.7.
Shell U.K. Ltd: 11.12.
Speedo (Europe) Ltd: 8.7b.
Dr James Stewart, Pathology Department, Postgraduate Medical School: 14.6a, 14.6b.
Syndication International Ltd: 12.1.
Thorn EMI Domestic Electrical Appliances Ltd: 8.8c.
Tropical Child Health Unit, Institute of Child Health: 13.9.
Van den Berghs & Jurgens Ltd: 2.11, 15.10, 15.11.
War on Want: 5.18, 5.19, 5.20.
Wellcome Institute Library, London: 1.6.
Westminster Hospital Medical School: 10.12.
Dr Paul Wheater: 11.3.
Dr Douglas P. Wilson: 6.6b.

Tables 1.2, 1.3, and 1.4 are from *National Food Survey*, Ministry of Agriculture, Fisheries, and Food.
Table 2.1 is from Open University (1978) *Food production systems* (T273). Open University.
Tables 3.1, 12.1, and 12.3 are from Paul, A.A., and Southgate, D.A.T. (1978) McCance and Widdowson's *The composition of foods*. 4th edition. H.M.S.O.
Table 6.2 is from Platt, B.S. (1962) *Tables of representative values of foods commonly used in tropical countries*. Medical Research Council special report series. H.M.S.O.
Figure 8.9 and table 12.2 is from *Food facts* Ministry of Agriculture, Fisheries, and Food.
Figure 8.13 is adapted from D.H.S.S. (1978) *Prevention and health — eating for health*. H.M.S.O.
Table 10.2 is adapted from D.H.S.S. (1980) *Rickets and osteomalacia*. Reports on health and social subjects. No. 19. H.M.S.O.

Table 12.4 is from Hughes, R.E. (1981) 'Vitamin C function, intake, and requirements'. *Proceedings of vitamin C symposium*. Applied Science Publishers.
Figure 13.8 is from Simpson, K.L. (1983) 'Relative value of carotenoids as precursors of vitamin A'. *Proceedings of the Nutrition Society*. 42. 7 — 17.
Figure 15.12 is from Heller, R.F., Heyward, D., and Hobbs, M.S.T. (1983) 'Decline in the rate of deaths from ischemic heart disease in the United Kingdom'. *British Medical Journal*. **286**. 260—2.
Table 15.2 is from Royal College of Physicians of London and British Cardiac Society (1976) 'Prevention of coronary heart disease'. *Journal of the Royal College of Physicians*. 10. 213 —75.

Illustrations by Beverly Levy, Rodney Paull, and Christopher Marshall.

Cover illustration by Robin Dodd.

Tables by Nina Konrad.

Introduction

What makes you choose the foods you eat? How can you find out about foods likely to keep you healthy? How much do you need to eat to keep your body working? Why is 'just enough' for some 'too much' for others? Are present-day eating habits responsible for national health problems? Does healthy eating mean giving up all the foods you enjoy and sticking to a dull unsatisfying diet?

Nutrition helps you answer these and other important questions. The investigations will help you understand how scientific research is undertaken, and why surveys and data collections are necessary as well as experiments.

People with a knowledge and understanding of nutrition can help not only themselves and their families but other people as well. They are needed in catering, the food industry, and the health professions. Getting across the message of good nutrition requires communication skills. *Nutrition* gives lots of practice in presenting information clearly and convincingly. It also encourages you to take a critical look at the use of nutritional information in advertising.

By the end of this course you should have found out a lot about what you should eat and why. In *Food Science* you can learn about the processing and cooking of food before you eat it.

CHAPTER 1
Why, where, and what do we eat?

Figure 1.1
The flow of food from field to table:
a *harvesting Brussels sprouts*
b *wholesale market*
c *school meals*
d *family meal*
e *food manufacturer*
f *supermarket.*

1.1
WHO NEEDS TO KNOW WHAT WE EAT?
Look at the photographs in figure 1.1 and the flowchart in figure 1.2. They show the flow of food from field to table.

Q 1
a Who is interested in knowing what we eat at each stage in the production of food?
b What 'interest' does each of these people have?

Q 2
a Who else is interested in knowing what you eat?
b Why is this knowledge useful to them?

Information is needed about people's food habits — what they eat and when and where they eat it. The only way to obtain this is to ask a lot of questions. But lots of individual answers are not very useful. They need to be combined to give us some general answers. This is the *survey* method of getting information.

Q 3
Have you carried out a survey before? If so, what did you find out?

A survey carried out in your class can quickly provide information about meal patterns.

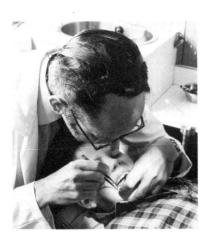

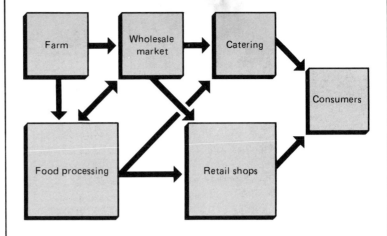

Figure 1.2

1.2
MEAL PATTERN SURVEYS
When and where is food eaten?

Food is eaten in two main ways.

1 Several foods are eaten together as a meal at more or less fixed times of day (for example, breakfast, lunch or dinner, an evening meal).

2 Only one or two foods are eaten as a snack between meals, or sometimes instead of a meal.

Think about the food you had yesterday.

Draw a table like the one in figure 1.4 and use it to record class totals (from a count of hands) for the meals and snacks eaten during the previous 24 hours. The totals can be sub-divided according to the places where the meals or snacks were eaten. To make it easier to compare the figures, work out the class results as percentages.

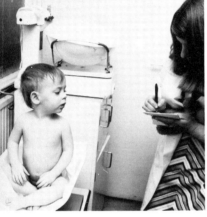

Figure 1.3
Interested in what you eat:
a *dentist*
b *doctor.*

Figure 1.4

Meal or snack (Number in class =)	Number eating meal	%	Where eaten:					
			home		school		out	
			number	%	number	%	number	%
Breakfast (6.00 a.m. to 9.30 a.m)								
Snack between breakfast and lunch								
Lunch (12.00 a.m. to 2.00 p.m.)								
Snack between lunch and tea								
Tea or evening meal (4.30 p.m. to 8.00 p.m.)								
Snack or supper								

This simple survey is a *24-hour recall survey* for meal patterns. It should give you a good idea of what the meal pattern is like for yourself and for your class as a whole. It shows you how many people in your class eat meals, snacks, or both. It will also show where these are eaten.

Q 4

What percentage of your class did not eat breakfast yesterday?

Q 5

What percentage had a midday meal in school?

The answers which can be obtained from such a survey would be a lot more useful if more people had taken part.

A survey like yours has been carried out by pupils in a school in Bath. Compare your figures with the results they obtained.

Meal		Percentages
Breakfast	Pupils having breakfast (cooked or cereal and toast)	85
	Pupils having no breakfast	15
Lunch	Pupils having lunch at school	80
	Pupils having lunch at home	15
	Pupils having lunch out	1
	Pupils having no lunch	4
Tea or evening meal	Pupils having a substantial meal	72
	Pupils having a snack meal	21
	Pupils having no meal	7

Table 1.1
Meal patterns of some pupils in Bath.

Q 6

How did your breakfast eating compare with the pupils in Bath?

Q 7

What about midday meals? From the information you have, can you say whether school dinners are as popular in your school as they are in Bath?

Q 8

You know which day of the week your results came from but you don't know this for the Bath results. Does this matter?

1.3
WHAT DO YOU LIKE TO EAT?
Another type of survey may tell you whether a lot of people or just a few people *like* a particular food. This is called a *food preference survey*. Look at the list of foods in worksheet NM1 which

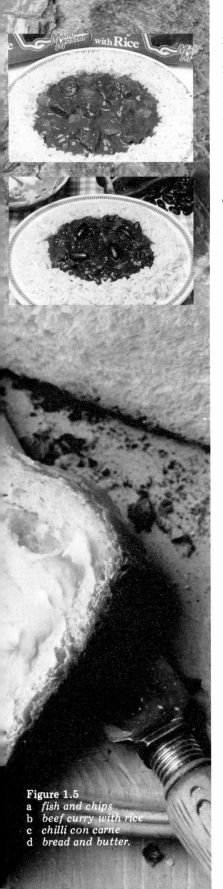

Figure 1.5
a *fish and chips*
b *beef curry with rice*
c *chilli con carne*
d *bread and butter.*

might be served for a main meal (like school dinner or lunch on a Sunday). Fill in the survey by putting ticks in one of the columns next to the food. If you like the food, tick the column marked 'like'. If you neither like nor dislike the food (in other words, you would eat the food if it were served, but not with any special pleasure) tick the column marked 'indifferent'. If you dislike the food and would not eat it at all if you could avoid it, tick the column marked 'dislike'.

Comparing likes and dislikes for foods — or for anything else — is difficult. How can you explain how much more you like ice-cream than, say, rice pudding? And yet preferences for certain foods are what make people buy them. If results can be given numerical values, they can be compared. Try working out preference ratios for the foods on worksheet NM1 for all the pupils in your class.

1 Find class totals for 'dislike', 'indifferent', and 'like' for each of the foods on worksheet NM1.

2 Calculate the preference ratio for each food using the formula below. A calculator will help with the calculation.

The number of people who *dislike* the food = d
The number of people who are *indifferent* to the food = i
The number of people who *like* the food = L

$$\text{The preference ratio} = \frac{1}{2}\left(\frac{L-d}{d+L+i}\right) + 1$$

Your teacher may show you some figures so that you can compare your class's results with those obtained in some primary schools in Sheffield.

Q 9
a Which type of food had the highest preference ratio?
b Why do you think that this was?

Q 10
a Which type of food had the lowest preference ratio?
b Why do you think that this was?

People usually tend to like foods which are sweet and contain sugar: jam sponge pudding and ice-cream probably had a fairly high preference ratio for your class. Most people also like fried and roast foods, which are cooked in fat or oil.

Foods are liked or disliked because of their odour (smell), flavour, colour, and texture. These are called *organoleptic* properties and are discussed in *Food science*, Chapter 3. In some countries, people are indifferent to their bland 'staple' food (for example, rice, bread, pasta, or some other cereal-based food) but they like the meat, fish, or other flavoursome foods served with the staple as sauces, stews, or spreads. These add interest to the meal as well as improving the nutritional value.

Look at the photographs in figure 1.5. Each shows two food items.

Q 11

Which food is the large quantity in each photograph?

Q 12

Which food is cheaper out of the pair in each photograph?

Q 13

Which food is the staple?

Q 14

For the staple food items, which two had the highest preference ratios? Why do you think this is?

You have looked at a staple food's properties. A staple is a food that is cheap and is eaten regularly in large quantities. It also contributes an important amount of energy and nutrients to the diet.

1.4
FINDING OUT ABOUT WHAT WE EAT

The first dietary survey in Britain was carried out in 1863 by a doctor called Edward Smith. The government paid him to find out about the diet of people who worked in the cotton industry in Lancashire. This industry was in a poor state and many workers were unemployed. In those days, with no unemployment pay, this meant semi-starvation or the workhouse.

Q 15

What do you think the government wanted to know?

Q 16

Why do you think the government wanted this information and how might they have used it?

Today, in Britain, the government still has a dietary survey — it is called the *National Food Survey* (N.F.S.). It is run by the Ministry of Agriculture, Fisheries, and Food.

The N.F.S. attempts to find out what families eat (food consumption) and how much they spend on food (food expenditure). *Food consumption* means food that is bought for use in a household. *Food expenditure* means all the money that is spent on food. Many different households from all over the country take part. The collection of information has gone on week after week and year after year since the N.F.S. was set up in 1944.

Each household is given a log-book. One member agrees to fill it in for one whole week. They fill in the description, the quantity, and the cost of food which enters the house to be eaten. The member also writes down the number of meals eaten outside the home and the amount of school milk consumed. A survey worker explains how to do this. Items not to be written down include takeaway foods eaten outside the home, sweets and chocolates, soft drinks, and alcohol.

Figure 1.6
Dr Edward Smith carried out the first dietary survey in Britain.

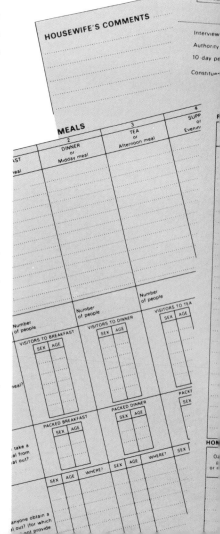

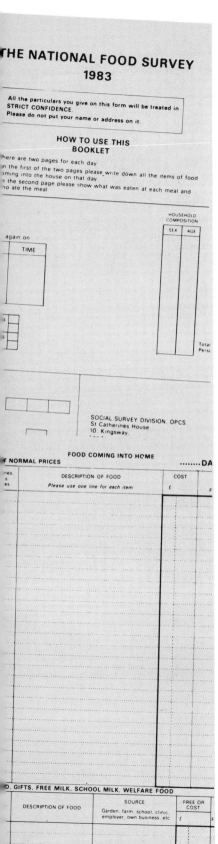

Figure 1.7
National food survey log-book.

Only families who agree to do this willingly take part. They are told that they won't be paid a fee and that their answers will be used confidentially. The N.F.S. is a very important source of information for all the groups of people mentioned in section 1.1. Families may refuse to take part in the survey. There is no penalty for refusing.

Q 17
Does the N.F.S. ask for weekly measurements of what the householder eats, what the householder's family eats, or what amount of food comes into the house?

Q 18
The survey worker calls at a house and asks the householder to take part in the survey.
a Will the householder be paid for taking part?
b Can householders refuse or will there be a fine if they do?

The N.F.S. is carried out all over Britain as it has to survey a *representative* sample. This means that, for instance, if 10 per cent of the whole population live in East Anglia, then 10 per cent of the households in the N.F.S. must come from East Anglia; and if 7 per cent of all the householders in Britain are old-age pensioners, then 7 per cent of the N.F.S. householders must be old-age pensioners.

Q 19
If 16 per cent of the population lives in Scotland, 50 per cent of all Scots earn between £100 and £150 per week, and the total number of survey householders is 8000, how many households in the survey should be Scots earning £100 to £150 per week?

Besides classifying households by region and income group, the N.F.S. also looks at differences between all-adult households and those with different numbers of children. There are also differences among families with different numbers of children to be considered. Table 1.2 shows you something about the income groups in the survey of 1979.

	Households with more than one earner					Households without an earner	
Gross weekly income of head of household	£200 and over	£145 and under £200	£90 and under £145	£56 and under £90	less than £56	£56 or more	less than £56
Class	A1	A2	B	C	D	E1	E2
Number of households	225	438	2168	1992	638	244	539

Table 1.2
N.F.S. household and income groups.

1.5
USING RESULTS FROM THE N.F.S.

Table 1.3 shows combinations of numbers of adults and children in households. For example, 10.4 per cent of households have 2 adults and 1 child.

Table 1.3
Combinations of adults and children in N.F.S. households.

Number of adults	Number of children	Number of each category	Percentage of all households
1	0	1211	16.7
	1 or more	200	2.7
2	0	2265	31.1
	1	756	10.4
	2	1120	15.4
	3	333	4.6
	4 or more	125	1.7
3	0	548	7.5
3 or more	1 or 2	456	6.3
	3 or more	100	1.4
4 or more	0	161	2.2
Total of all household types		7275	100

Q 20
Which two sizes of household (numbers of adults and children) are most common?

Worksheets NM2 and NM3 show you some of the results from the N.F.S. They deal with food consumption and expenditure classified by *family size*. Notice that all the data are 'per person per week'.

1 Make a table with the same headings and lines as those in worksheet NM2.

2 For each 'total', find which household size consumed *most* of that food. Put a '+' in the table. Then find which household consumed *least* and put a '−' in the table.

Figure 1.8 The table will look like figure 1.8.

Household size	adults		1		2				
	children	0	1 or more	0	1	2	3	4 or more
Total milk and cream		+						
Total cheese		+						−
Total meat								−

3 Now make another table in the same way using the information on worksheet NM3. This shows the *amount of money* spent on different kinds of food per person.

Q 21
Do your two tables match up? If not, write down some reasons why they are different.

Q 22
Using worksheet NM3, work out the total expenditure on food per person, and per household, for households of:

1 adult and no children
2 adults and no children
2 adults and 1 child
2 adults and 3 children
3 adults and no children.

Q 23
Which household size spent the most?

Discuss these results with your teachers. Think about the age of the children, the amount they need to eat, and how much adults need to eat.

BACKGROUND READING

THE BRITISH DIET
Food habits vary all over the World. The Italians are famous for their pasta, the French for their cheese and wine, and the Germans for their sausages. In Britain, the National Food Survey tells us a lot about our food habits. For instance, as a nation we drink twice as much milk and eat far more lamb than most other European countries. Our consumption of wine, cheese, fruit, and vegetables is amongst the lowest in Europe.

Table 1.4
National food habits: food supplies in kg per person per year.

	United Kingdom	France	West Germany	Italy
Milk, liquid	145	65	59	56
Cheese	6	15	10	11
Meat:	74	97	89	65
beef and veal	24	30	23	25
mutton and lamb	8	3	1	1
pig meat	26	33	50	17
poultry	12	14	9	15
Potatoes	99	95	92	37
Other vegetables	75	115	70	153
Fruit	48	79	116	108
Sugar, refined	46	38	36	29
Visible fats	22	24	25	23
Wheat	64	70	47	129
Wine (litres)	6	103	23	103
Beer (litres)	114	46	147	16

We can also see from the survey that there are strong regional likes and dislikes for particular foods within Britain. Londoners tend to buy far more fresh green vegetables and fruit and drink more coffee than the average Scotsman or Welshmen; while the Welsh, unlike the rest of country, prefer salty butter to margarine. Some areas have their own local traditional foods that have been popular for centuries. Meat-pie, sausages, black pudding (blood sausage), and tripe (part of cow, sheep, or ox stomach) are still doing a brisk trade in the Midlands and North of England.

Food habits do change and the National Food Survey shows this up quite well. It shows how over the last 30 years the British have cut down on bread, fish, and sugar, and started to buy more cheese and vegetables. Higher vegetable sales have certainly been helped by recent advances in food science. Processes such as canning and quick-freezing have meant that vegetables can now be bought out of season.

The N.F.S. also shows how the British are now able to enjoy a vast choice of foreign cuisines. Very few people in India will ever sample the delights of 'Sunday roast beef', but most people here will taste a curry at some time in their lives. Although travel abroad has done a lot to widen our tastes, immigration to the United Kingdom has done far more. Small shops have sprung up everywhere to meet the needs of immigrant communities. Up until the 1950s Chinese food was virtually unknown in Britain — now almost every high street has a Chinese takeaway. Add to this the kebab houses, pizzerias, and American hamburger restaurants and it shouldn't surprise you to learn that of all the money spent by the British public on food prepared outside the home, more than 20 per cent is now spent in foreign restaurants and takeaways.

Figure 1.9
Eating out in foreign restaurants has widened people's tastes.

CHAPTER 2

What is food?

2.1
TALKING ABOUT FOOD

Probably most people talk, read, or hear about food in some way every day of their lives. They might be discussing likes and dislikes, shopping for food, or ordering a meal in a restaurant. You often see or hear food advertisements. Articles on food appear frequently in newspapers and magazines.

So many people with so much to say about food! Surely they must know what food is. Do you?

Q 1

What is your definition of a food?

Compare your answers with dictionary definitions. Not all correct answers will be the same. Some will say that a food is something which is taken in by the mouth and creates a pleasing sensation. Others think it doesn't matter how food gets into the body as long as, once inside, it's useful. But what do we mean by 'useful'?

Once you have settled on your definition, use it to decide which items in figure 2.2 are foods.

Q 2

Which are foods? Which are non-foods? Give reasons for your decisions based on your definition.

BRANIES
SACCHARINE
ASPIRIN
VITAMIN C

Figure 2.2

Figure 2.1
So much to say about food!

HOW TURKEY BECAME OUR CELEBRATIO BIRD
Farmhouse Cheese
Temporibud autem quins
Slimming
meat
Versatile eggs

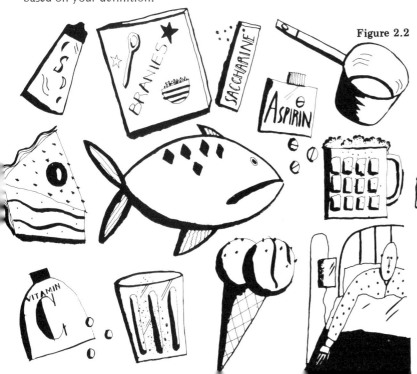

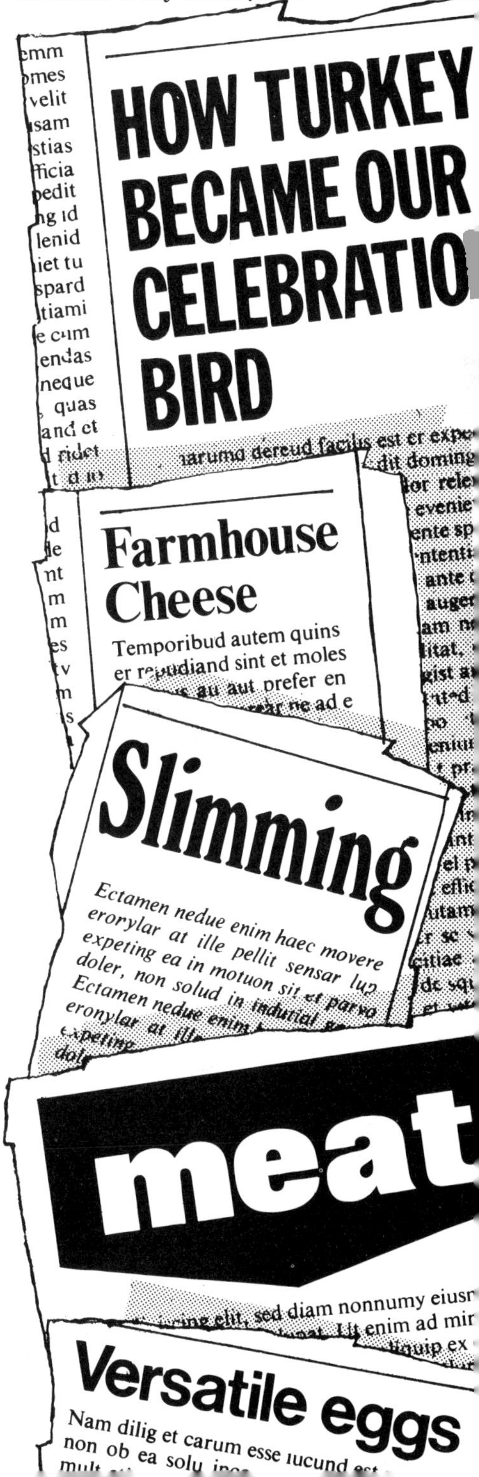

How useful was your definition for deciding between foods and non-foods? You may need to alter it. When you have studied later chapters, which are about the uses of foods to the body, you may want to alter it yet again.

2.2
CLASSIFYING FOODS
Once people have agreed about definitions, they can exchange information. The advantage of writing your own definition for something as ordinary as food is that it makes you think clearly and gives you a good starting point for further studies. Because there are so many different foods, they can only be studied by grouping similar foods together — that is by classifying them. This means agreeing on definitions for the *generic* names given to groups of foods. (A generic name is a name for a group of similar things.)

Everyone who works with foods classifies them. The supermarket manager puts up notices to help us to find what we want. Everyone knows what comes into groups headed 'vegetables', 'meat', and 'fats', but what about 'preserves'? This includes jams and pickles but not other kinds of preserved foods such as canned and frozen foods.

Some generic food names become less useful as shopping habits change. Years ago, shops called 'dairies' were common. Could you name the foods which would be sold there? These are still called 'dairy foods' in some textbooks. Other names are introduced, some from abroad, some by new fashions. Would you know what you could expect to find in a delicatessen and in a health food store?

Look at your food tables (worksheet M21).

Q 3
How many generic food names are used?

Q 4
Why is it useful to have foods classified like this?

Q 5
In what order are foods in each group listed?

Look back at your copy of figure 1.8.

Q 6
a Which generic food names are used?
b How complete a classification is this? (Try to think of foods which would not fit into these groups.)
c Why is it necessary to limit the number of groups in a table like this?

In Chapter 1 the generic word 'staple' was defined (see section 1.3).

Figure 2.3
Classifying foods.

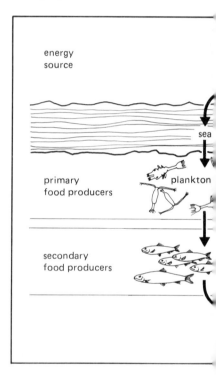

Figure 2.5

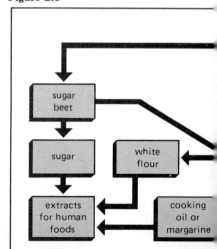

Figure 2.4
Two food chains.

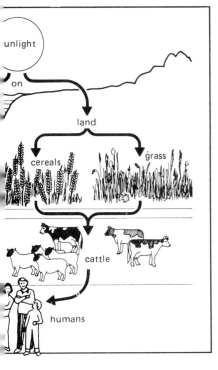

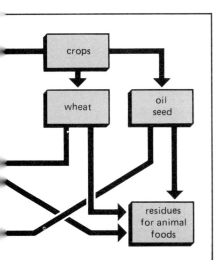

Q 7
What definitions would you give for the non-staple parts of the main meals shown on worksheet NM1?

2.3
SOURCES OF FOOD
One of the most important classifications divides foods into just two groups: foods from *plants* and foods from *animals*.

Q 8
What names are given to people who choose to eat:
a no foods from animals
b no foods from slaughtered animals?

Q 9
What are their reasons?

People who wish to avoid eating food from animals need to know about the sources of foods.

Q 10
a Which of the following come from plants and which from animals?

cornflour	spaghetti	lard	peanuts
gelatin	margarine	sugar	cooking oil
honey	marmite	yoghurt	semolina
mince	mincemeat	tripe	kipper

b Can you be sure about all of them?
c Look back to your answer to question 2. Are there any substances which you decided were foods which do not come either from plants or from animals?

Nearly all foods or materials which go into prepared foods come from either plants or animals. Green plants take in sunlight energy and make their own food. Animals cannot do this; they have to eat plants or animals. Therefore all food production begins with plants. Figure 2.4 shows two food chains.

Q 11
What process occurs in green plants which cannot take place in animals?

Q 12
What is passed from the sun to animals via green plants?

Q 13
Name the different human foods that can be obtained by rearing cattle.

Q 14
Name other animals (not just mammals) which are reared for the food they provide for humans.

Many farmers do not depend on grass alone for feeding their animals. In winter, when grass is scarce, cattle and poultry foods are used to keep up milk and egg production. Left-overs from the processing of food for humans can be used to make animal foodstuffs as shown in figure 2.5.

In the more prosperous countries of the World, cereal crops such as barley are grown specially for feeding beef cattle. Young animals fed with cereals instead of grass grow quickly, and when slaughtered their meat is of high quality. Some people object to cereal crops being used to feed animals, particularly when there are food shortages in many parts of the World. They argue that more food would be available if farmers stopped producing meat and grew crops for human food instead.

Table 2.1 shows how many people could get enough protein from one hectare of land (approximately 2 football pitches) when it is used to produce different foods. Remember that these figures are only estimates and that some land which can be used for grazing animals could not be ploughed for wheat. But they do show a big difference between amounts of protein which can come from plant crops and from meat production.

Food	Number of people per hectare
Beef (cattle)	0.46
Wheat	3.17
Rice	4.65
Soya	13.39

Table 2.1
Protein productivity and land use.

Before we can think about the nutritional consequences of switching to a diet which includes more plant food and less animal food we need to know how they differ.

2.4
DIFFERENCES BETWEEN PLANT AND ANIMAL CELLS
Many foods consist of portions of plant or animal tissue. These are made up of large numbers of tiny cells packed together. There are very many different kinds of cells but *all* cells have some features in common, and all plant cells differ in some ways from all animal cells. Look at particular examples of plant and animal cells magnified by a microscope and identify the features shown in the simplified diagrams of typical plant and animal cells in figure 2.6.

IIII YOU WILL NEED: IIIIIIIIIIIIIIIIIIIIIIIIIIIIIIIIIIIIIIIIIIIIIIIIIIIIIIIIIIIIIIIIIIIIIIIIIIIIIIIIII

Small segment of raw onion
Water
Worksheet M27
Compound microscope

2 slides and coverslips
Mounted needle
Clean spatula or teaspoon

1 Take some cells from the inside of your cheek by scraping gently with a clean spatula.

2 Transfer the cells to a clean microscope slide. Add a drop of water and a coverslip as shown on worksheet M27.

3 Examine the slide under the microscope. Draw what you see.

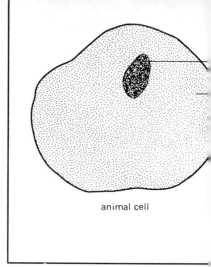
animal cell

Figure 2.6
Simplified animal and plant cells.

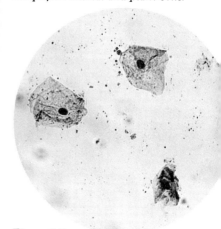

Figure 2.7
Photomicrographs of:
a *cheek cells*

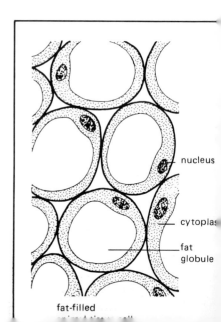
nucleus

cytoplas

fat globule

fat-filled

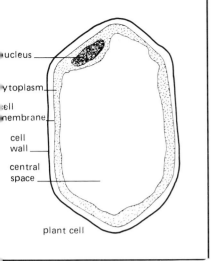

plant cell

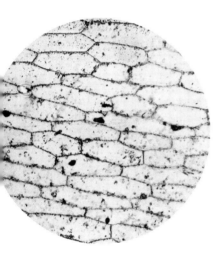

b *onion cells.*

Figure 2.8
Food stores in animal and plant cells.

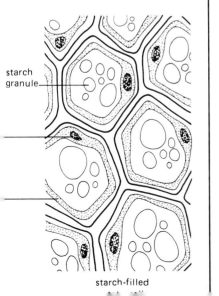

starch-filled

4 Separate the layers of your onion and take a small piece of the fine skin found in between.

5 Spread this out on a microscope slide. Add a drop of water and a coverslip. Examine the slide under the microscope.

6 Draw what you see. Compare your drawings of actual cells with the diagrams in figure 2.6 which have been simplified to show the main features clearly. Label those features shown in figure 2.6 on your own drawings.

Q 15
What features are common to both animal and plant cells?

Q 16
What features are shown by plant cells only?

Differences between plant and animal cells cause differences in plant and animal tissues used for food.

1 Plant tissues contain the stiff cell wall materials (mainly cellulose) called dietary fibre. Animal tissues do not.
2 Both plant and animal tissues contain cytoplasm and are sources of the proteins and other chemicals which cytoplasm contains. But plant cells contain a lot of water in their central spaces and therefore less cytoplasm.

Another difference, which cannot be seen, concerns the food stores of plants and animals. The main store in plants is starch. This forms as granules in the central space in the cells of potato tubers and seeds, such as cereals, peas, and beans.

Animal cells do not store starch. They lay down fat in fatty tissue cells. These enlarge as they fill up with fat so that the cytoplasm and nucleus are are pushed to the side (see figure 2.8). Some plants store fat as oil, usually in their seeds, but there is still less fat than starch.

Q 17
Name two substances which are present in plant tissue foods but not in animal tissue foods.

The important chemicals in cytoplasm are present in both plant and animal tissues when used for food. These are the nutrients in foods.

Q 18
Why are animal tissues more concentrated sources of nutrients than plant tissues?

The energy from the sun is stored by plants (mainly in starch) and animals (mainly in fat). Fat is a more concentrated source of energy than starch.

Q 19
Give *two* reasons why people depending on plant foods need to eat a larger bulk of food than people who eat a mixture of plant and animal foods.

Figure 2.9
What have these animals in common?
a *cows*
b *hens*
c *bees.*

2.5
SPECIAL PURPOSE FOODS
Look at figure 2.9.

Q 20
a What have these animals in common?
b Why are they able to contribute to the supply of foods for humans?

Foods produced by animals for the special purpose of feeding their young must be rich sources of nutrients; humans can make good use of them. Our bodies have similar structures to those of cows and hens so it is reasonable to expect that cows' milk and eggs will provide many of the nutrients we need. Honey is not the only food supplied for nourishing the larvae of bees and the range of nutrients it contains is limited.

Although eggs and cows' milk are valuable, it should be remembered that they are intended for the young of other species and are not *essential* in the diets of humans.

Q 21
What food is provided naturally for human babies? If this is not available, an artificial food must be made and dried cows' milk is usually part of this.

2.6
REFINED AND UNREFINED FOODS
Figure 2.5 shows how some food crops are separated into 'extracts' for human foods and 'residues' for animals foods. This is called 'refining'. Sugar, white flour, and cooking oil are called *refined foods*. Foods which consist of whole tissues (or secretions) of plants or animals are called *unrefined foods*.

Q 22
Which of the foods listed in question 10 are refined and which unrefined?

Q 23
Make a list of the refined foods and the unrefined foods from which each comes.

Food is not refined in order to make animal feedstuff. Residues are used because they are available. Manufacturers refine food for several reasons; for example:

1 Refined sugar will keep for years but sugar beet will rot in a few months.
2 White flour makes loaves which have a lighter texture and a larger volume than wholemeal flour.
3 Polished rice looks more attractive when boiled than brown rice.

But, refining can waste useful sources of nutrients. Figure 2.10 shows the parts of the wheat grain which are removed when white flour is milled. The bran layers and wheat germ are better sources of some nutrients than the endosperm (see table 2.2).

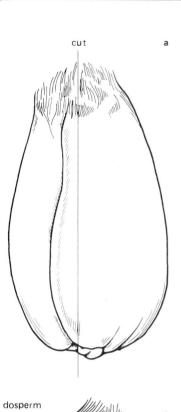

cut   a

Nutrient (per 100 g)	Endosperm, bran, and germ	Endosperm only
Protein (g)	13.2	11.3
Fat (g)	2.0	1.2
Sugars (g)	2.3	1.5
Starch (g)	57.0	67.0
Dietary fibre (g)	9.6	3.0
Thiamin (mg)	0.46	0.1
Calcium (mg)	35.0	15.0
Iron (mg)	4.0	1.5

Table 2.2
The effect of milling on the nutrient content of wheat.

Wholemeal flour is made from the whole of the wheat grains: the endosperm, the bran, and the germ. White flour is endosperm only.

Q 24
Which nutrients are reduced to a half or less when white (refined) flour is produced?

When millers put back into white flour vitamins and minerals up to the levels in wholemeal flour, they are carrying out *nutrient restoration.*

Doctors are concerned that many people in this country do not get enough dietary fibre.

Q 25
How many times more dietary fibre are you likely to get from wholemeal bread than from white bread?

Several other vitamins and minerals are present in larger amounts in unrefined wholemeal flour than in refined white flour. Their importance in the diet might be greater than we think.

It is not only the manufacturer who wastes valuable nutrients. Often we remove edible and nutritional parts during food preparation. The skins of apples and potatoes are nutritious and tasty yet many people throw them away. People get used to refined foods and think that they prefer the taste and texture. It is possible that they would enjoy the unrefined foods just as much, or even more, if they were given a chance to try them. In your next practical session try using some unrefined foods to replace normal refined ingredients. This should be a way of making better use of available food and avoiding waste. But remember that your food must always be appetizing and tasty or it will not be eaten — and then it will all be wasted!

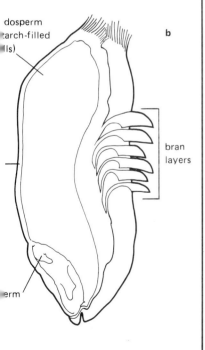

dosperm
tarch-filled
lls)   b

bran layers

erm

Figure 2.10
a   *wheat grain showing direction of cross-section in* b
b   *cross-section showing layers of bran peeled back.*

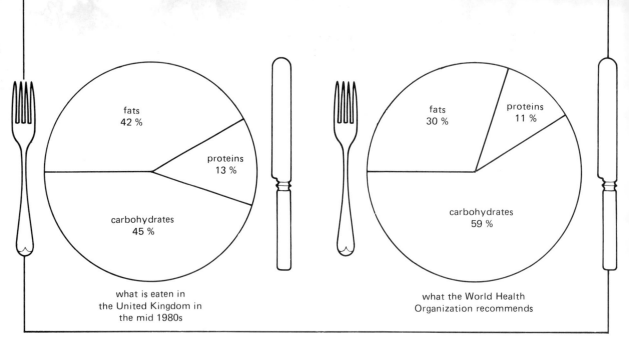

Figure 2.11

BACKGROUND READING

THE BATTLE FOR DIETARY GOALS

Dietary goals are precise statements of changes needed in the average diet of a community to bring about better health.
The first country to start the argument of setting dietary goals was the United States. In 1968 a select Senate committee was set up to investigate hunger and malnutrition amongst the poor. Almost ten years later they had to conclude that they were faced with more widespread nutrition problems. It became clear that a healthy diet involves more than just the satisfaction of nutrient needs — it also has to limit certain foods which may be harmful if eaten in large quantities.

The report, called 'Dietary goals for the United States', was published in 1977. It recommended that Americans should eat less fat, cholesterol, salt, and sugar, and more fibre. To achieve these goals the report advised people to eat less meat and more fish and poultry; substitute high-fat dairy products with low-fat alternatives; and eat fewer eggs and more fruits, vegetables, and whole grains.

The reaction to the report came quickly. Farm groups and senators representing agricultural states were quick to demand the report be withdrawn. Senators were told they were at risk in future elections if they supported the dietary goals idea. More debate followed. Committees of experts looked at the evidence and agreed with the dietary goals. Eventually it took a Senate committee to make the Government listen and to begin to act. Americans have started to make the changes that took so long to be accepted.

The same story is being repeated in the United Kingdom. In 1973, the Department of Health and Social Security stated that an improvement in nutrition education was needed. The National Advisory Committee on Nutrition Education (N.A.C.N.E.) was set up five years later.

N.A.C.N.E. reported that the average British diet is not a healthy one. Its recommendations for change are for everyone, not just for those 'at risk' or ill. The present British diet is the result of changing lifestyles, the productivity of our farmers, and the activities of the food industry. The report states that many meat and dairy products are too high in fat. It says that snacks and fast foods should be available that do not contain excessive fat, salt, or sugar. It recommends major changes in food manufacturing and marketing. It says that food should be labelled in such a way that people know what they are buying.

The N.A.C.N.E. guidelines for the United Kingdom (see worksheet NM19) give general advice without suggesting dramatic changes. However, some people taking the advice will find that their diet needs much more alteration than others. A major benefit of all the argument is the awareness of nutrition it has stimulated in the public, the government, and the food industry.

The battle will probably be a long one if the American experience is anything to go by. Victory in the battle will lead to better health for the individual and the community at large.

CHAPTER 3

Animal, vegetable, and mineral

3.1
FOODS CONTAIN CHEMICALS

Like all materials, foods are made of chemicals. The ones which the body uses are called *nutrients*. About fifty different nutrients must be provided by the diet to keep the body in good working order.

Information about nutrient composition of foods can be found in food tables and on the packets or labels of some manufactured foods. Other chemicals in foods can be useful even if they are not nutrients. These are the chemicals which give food its colours, flavours, and textures, making it more interesting to eat. Certain chemicals, both nutrient and non-nutrient, can be harmful if eaten in excess. A good diet supplies the wide range of nutrients in the amounts needed and avoids too much of any one nutrient.

Q 1
Which are more likely to supply a wide range of nutrients, refined foods or unrefined foods? Explain your answer and give *two* examples.

Q 2
Most foods contain several nutrients. A few contain only one. Find three single-nutrient foods in the food tables (worksheet M21). How were these foods obtained?

Q 3
The food tables in the book *The composition of foods* give information about all the fifty nutrients. Those on worksheet M21 only give ten. Suggest reasons for this. Why do you think these ten were chosen?

Most of the nutrients needed in the diet will be provided if a wide variety of foods is eaten, including some unrefined foods. Problems linked to intakes of nutrients occur for two reasons.

1 When people are not getting enough food in total.
2 When people are getting too much of a particular nutrient.

The dietary guidelines referred to in Chapter 2 aim to solve current nutritional problems affecting the health of the community in Britain. They help by highlighting certain nutrients which need to be increased or reduced in the diets of most people.

Q 4
a Which nutrients have been highlighted?
b For each nutrient, state whether intakes should be increased or reduced.

INGREDIENTS:
100% Whole Wheat

✓ Natural Wholewheat w WHEATGERM and BRAN retained

✓ Source of Natural Fibre

✓ Energy value: —
1505 kilojoules per 100g
(350 calories per 100

✓ **NO ADDED SUGAR**

✓ **NO ADDED SALT**

Figure 3.1
Cereal packets showing two ways of displaying nutrient composition.

OBESITY HEART DISEASE   *BETTER HEALTH*

LOW SALT

LOW FAT

Kellogg's
CRUNCHY NUT
CORN FLAKES
THE BEST TO YOU ™

Ingredients:
Maize, brown sugar, peanuts, sugar, honey, salt, malt, niacin, iron, vitamin B$_6$, riboflavin, thiamin, vitamin D$_3$.

Typical Nutritional Composition per 100 grammes

Energy	372 kcal
	1560 kJ
Protein (N × 6.25)	7.7 g
Vitamins:	
Niacin	16.0 mg
Vitamin B$_6$	1.8 mg
Riboflavin (B$_2$)	1.5 mg
Thiamin (B$_1$)	1.0 mg
Vitamin D$_3$	2.8 μg
Iron	6.7 mg

A serving of 30 g of Kellogg's Crunchy Nut Corn Flakes provides at least a quarter of the average adult or a third of a child's recommended intake of these vitamins; and one-sixth of their iron needs.

Figure 3.2

3.2
HOW MUCH FAT ARE YOU EATING?

Often you can tell when you are eating fat. This is because fat won't mix with water on the skin or tongue, giving a sensation of greasiness. Some fats can be seen. Examples are fat layers on meat and extracted fats, and oils such as butter from milk and olive oil from olives. Fats which are easily recognized either by touch or sight are called *visible* fats.

The amounts of visible fats which people eat can vary greatly. How much fat is there in a ham sandwich?

|||| YOU WILL NEED: ||||||||||||||||||||||||||||||||||||||||||||||||||||||||||||||||||||||||

2 slices of bread	Knife
Soft margarine	Fork
Slice of boiled ham (including	Kitchen paper
the fat) wrapped in cling film	Lever arm balance (to 250 g)

1 Weigh two slices of bread on a sheet of kitchen paper to the nearest gram.

2 Spread each slice with margarine, keeping the bread on the paper to avoid losing any crumbs.

3 Reweigh the bread and work out how much margarine was used.

4 Examine the ham without removing the cling film and decide whether you would:
remove all the fat, *or*
remove about half the fat, *or*
remove no fat
before making the sandwich.

5 *One* member of the group should then unwrap the ham, trim off the fat, and weigh it.

6 Those who decided to remove no fat should add the total weight of ham fat to the weight of margarine they used. Those who decided to remove half the fat should add half the weight of ham fat to the weight of margarine.

Discuss the results with your teacher.

Q 5
a What are the highest and lowest amounts of fat in ham sandwiches according to your class's results? Are these exact results or only estimations?
b Why would it be useful to know the average amount of fat in ham sandwiches?

Following the dietary guideline to cut down fats means spreading margarine or butter thinly and trimming off visible fat. Another approach would be to use a low-fat spread.

How much fat do low-fat spreads contain and how do they compare with other table and cooking fats?

Variety of solid fats

Boiling-tubes of equal size
(one for each fat)
Boiling-tube rack

Water bath *or* saucepan covered
with wire netting
Labels
Chinagraph pencil
Access to cooker

1 Put a chinagraph pencil mark two-thirds of the way up each boiling-tube and leave them to stand in a warm place.

2 Fill each boiling-tube up to the mark with one of the fats. (Small pieces of fat will melt and run down into the warm tube.)

3 Label each boiling-tube with the name of the fat it contains and stand them upright in a water bath.

4 Heat at a simmer for 5 minutes. Remove the boiling-tubes to a rack.

5 Look for separate watery and oily layers. Measure d (total depth), f (depth of fatty layer), and w (depth of watery layer — if any) in millimetres.

6 Use the formula below to calculate the percentage of fat by volume.

Percentage of fat by volume = $\frac{f}{d} \times 100$

7 Compare the results for all the fats tested.

Q 6
How does low-fat spread compare with your table margarine? Could you reduce your fat intake just as well by spreading margarine (or butter) more thinly?

Q 7
How does your measurement of percentage fat by volume compare with percentage fat by weight calculated from the food tables?

3.3
WHICH ARE THE HIGH-FAT FOODS?
The trouble with a dietary guideline aimed at cutting down fat intakes is that most of us like fat. Even if you cut all the fat off your ham, you probably enjoy the flavours and textures which fat gives to cooked food. Turn back to the results of your preference ratio calculations (Chapter 1). It is very likely that chipped and roast potatoes came out higher than boiled or jacket potatoes.

If all fats were 'visible', we would always know which were high-fat foods. Unfortunately, a lot of fat in food is emulsified, that is, broken down into tiny droplets which mix with water. Oil droplets coated with water no longer feel greasy. Egg yolk and thickened sauces are good examples of emulsions with high 'invisible' fat content. Anyone advised by a doctor to eat less fat needs to learn which are the high-fat foods.

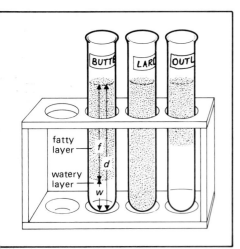

Figure 3.3

1 Copy the list of foods in figure 3.4. Tick the ones you *think* are high-fat foods.

Food	Fat (%)	Food	Fat (%)
Cheddar cheese		almonds	
cottage cheese		peanuts	
whipping cream		boiled potatoes	
whole milk		chipped potatoes	
boiled egg		potato crisps	
fried egg		milk chocolate	
grilled bacon		digestive biscuits	
grilled beefburger		pork pie	
cooked sausages		tomato & cheese pizza	
grilled fish fingers		ice-cream	

Figure 3.4

2 Now check using food tables. Beside each one, write the percentage of fat it contains. Work this out by changing grams of fat per portion to grams of fat per 100 g of food.

Q 8
Which three foods in the list have the highest percentage of fat? No doubt you ticked bacon, but did you expect almonds and peanuts to contain so much fat?

Q 9
What advice would you give to someone on a low-fat diet about eating potatoes?

Q 10
Several of the foods on the list were grilled. What would be the effect of frying on their percentage fat content?

Q 11
When comparing percentage fats in the foods in figure 3.4, why would it have been better to include whole milk powder (26.3 per cent fat) rather than whole liquid milk?

Figure 3.5

3.4
THE TASTY NUTRIENTS — SUGAR AND SALT
The sugar and salt in the food cupboard have quite a lot in common. Both are white crystalline water-soluble solids. They are easy to keep, measure, and mix with other foods. They add distinctive flavours to foods which are well liked. (Look how many sweet and salty foods are high on your preference ratio list.) Added in large amounts they help preserve foods. They are single-nutrient foods: sugar is sucrose and salt is sodium chloride. However, *both* are mentioned in dietary guidelines.

milk chocolate digestive sweetmeal biscuits 200 g

Ingredients: Flour, milk chocolate, vegetable and animal fat, sugar, wholemeal flour, cane syrup, raising agents (sodium bicarbonate, ammonium bicarbonate), salt.

Figure 3.6
Food labels showing the presence of sugar and salt in two manufactured foods.

Figure 3.7

For better health, in Britain and in other countries where food is plentiful, intakes of both sugar and salt need to be reduced. This can begin with less added from the salt cellar or the sugar basin to food and drinks at the table. The very distinctive flavours ought to help us avoid eating too much in cooked or manufactured foods.

How good are you at tasting sugar and salt?

1 Draw a table like figure 3.7. As you copy the list of foods, try to remember how each tastes.

Food	A Sweet, salty, or neither	B Sugar, g per portion	C Contains salt?
white bread			
cornflakes			
spaghetti, cooked			
cheese			
milk, whole			
fruit yoghurt			
liver, fried			
apple, eating			
banana			
carrots, boiled			
potatoes, boiled			
lemonade, bought			
cake, gingerbread			
biscuits, cream crackers			

2 In column A, state whether you remember each food as sweet, salty, or neither sweet nor salty.

3 Use the food tables (worksheet M21) to find the amounts of sugar per portion. Write these down in column B.

4 Salt is not shown in the food tables. But for most of the foods, you can find out whether salt is added when they are prepared or cooked by looking at recipes or packets. Tick in column C the foods which you know contain salt.

Q 12
Do all foods which contain sugar taste sweet and all food containing salt taste salty? How do you explain your findings?

Q 13
What other effects might sugar and salt have in food as well as making it sweet or salty?

Figure 3.8

Q 14
Sucrose added to cooked and processed foods is not the only sugar we eat. Which foods in figure 3.7 contain sugars naturally? Name the different sugars which are in these foods.

Sugars should not be thought of as necessarily harmful. The body regularly uses some sugar for its energy supply. Sugar is harmful when it is eaten in excessive amounts or by itself. Sugars eaten as they occur naturally are usually mixed with so many other materials that it would be difficult to get too much or have a concentrated sugar solution in the mouth.

Q 15
There is one natural food which is an exception to the above statement. What is it?

3.5
SALT: WHICH FOODS CONTRIBUTE MOST?
Food tables do not show amounts of salt. Some show amounts of sodium and chloride. These are the two parts into which salt splits when it dissolves in water. Adding salt to food increases both sodium and chloride. It is the amount of sodium getting into the body which affects health. Concern about salt in the diet should really be concern about sodium. Table 3.1 lists some common foods which have high concentrations of sodium (more than 450 mg per 100 g). To find which of them contribute most sodium to your diet, you need to know the size of an average portion *and* how often you are likely to eat it. For example, Marmite has a much higher concentration of sodium than bread has but you will probably eat only a teaspoon (10 g) of Marmite on a thick (50 g) slice of bread.

100 g Marmite contain 4500 mg sodium
10 g Marmite contain 450 mg sodium

100 g bread contain 540 mg sodium
50 g bread contain 270 mg sodium

Although there is more sodium in the Marmite than in the bread, you probably eat bread much more often than Marmite. Of course, if you never eat Marmite, it won't add any sodium to your diet!

Table 3.1
Some common foods which have high concentrations of sodium.

Food	mg sodium per 100 g	Food	mg sodium per 100 g
All Bran	1670	Salmon (canned)	570
Bread (white)	540	Sardines (canned,	
Bread (wholemeal)	550	drained)	650
Cornflakes	1160	Shrimps/prawns	3840
		Baked beans	480
Porridge	580	Potato (crisps)	550
Cheese (cheddar)	610	Biscuits	
Cheese (cottage)	450	(cream crackers)	610
Skimmed milk powder	550	Scones	800
Butter	870	Liver sausage	860
Margarine	820	Pork pie	720
Bacon, streaky		Shepherd's pie	510
(grilled)	1990	Steak and kidney pie	450
Bacon joint (boiled)	1100	Kedgeree	790
Beefburgers (grilled)	880	Soup (canned)	450
Corned beef	950	Table salt	38 850
Sausage (cooked)	1000	Marmite	4500
Kippers (cooked)	990	Bovril	4800

1 Pick out those foods from table 3.1 which you eat at least once a week.

2 Use the food tables (worksheet M21) to find the size of a usual portion. Some foods in table 3.1 are not included in the food tables. You will need to know the following portion weights: soup (one dish): 150 g; salt (one salt spoon): 5 g; Bovril (one beverage): 10 g.

3 Work out in mg the sodium per portion of the foods you eat frequently.

Q 16
Which foods contribute most sodium to your diet?

Q 17
Which foods ought to be avoided by anyone advised to cut down on salt?

3.6
LIKES AND DISLIKES
Dietary guidelines won't be followed if they take away the foods people like and leave the foods they don't enjoy. Food is only nutritious when it is eaten! The nutrients dealt with in this chapter all make food popular, but we are not asked to cut out fats, sugar, and salt, only to reduce our intakes. One way to cut down sugar is to use non-sugar sweeteners such as saccharine; another is to change our likes and dislikes. Do you know anyone who has given up sugar (or sweeteners) in tea and now prefers it unsweetened? Probably they had a struggle at

first but in time they succeeded in changing a food preference. Now they may well dislike tea containing sugar. Do you know anyone who always adds salt to their soup before even tasting it? This is a habit which could be changed.

Q 18

a How have Americans responded to the dietary goal to reduce sugar consumption? (See figure 3.9.)
b Have they lost their taste for sweet foods?

Try some recipes in which sugar content has been reduced, and then try to organize some food tasting panels to get some reactions to the results.

Figure 3.9
Graph showing changes in consumption of sugar and saccharine in the United States, 1972 to 1982.

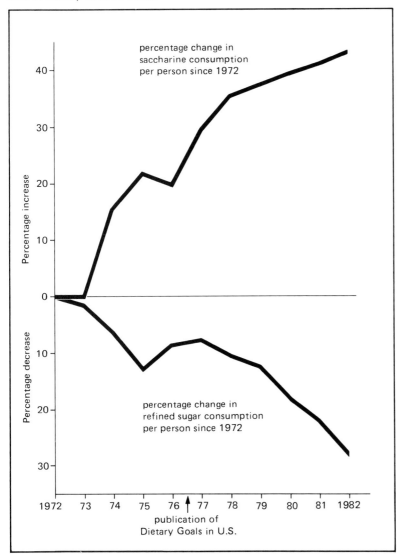

WHO NEEDS FAT?

Heart disease is very common in the rich industrial countries. Every year millions of pounds are spent on research to help us understand more about it. Studies have shown that sufferers have a high level of cholesterol in their blood and that too much fat in the diet may well be the cause. A recent survey found that the World's highest rates of heart disease occurred in east Finland and Glasgow in Scotland. It is in these places that people eat the most fat. Doctors and nutritionists agree that too much fat in the diet is a bad thing.

In poor countries, where people eat far less fat, heart disease is at a low level. On average, fat supplies only 15 per cent of the energy in the diet in poor countries compared with 40 per cent in rich countries. This is because fat-rich foods (*e.g.* meat, cheese, and oil) are too expensive for many people to buy. The bulk of the diet in developing countries is made up of cereal and other plant foods. Cereals are low in fat.

Just as we in the rich world should try and cut down on our fat intake, people in the developing world need more fat — especially in the diets of young children. One of the problems that growing infants have to face is the *weaning* period (when they learn to eat solid food). In poor countries, it is the time when malnutrition is most likely to occur.

The common weaning diet in poor countries is a gruel (porridge) made from a cereal or root crop, *e.g.* cassava. As the children can only take semi-solids during weaning, the cereal has to be diluted to about 95 per cent water so that it can be drunk. A one-year-old child must then drink about 4 litres a day to get his energy needs. This is a lot to ask of a small stomach, and unless the child can have small and frequent feeds he may well go short on energy.

One answer would be to put more fat and oil into weaning foods. Fat is a very concentrated energy source, about twice as concentrated as protein or carbohydrate. It also makes food less viscous (less solid), and therefore easier to swallow. If fat is added to a weaning food it would produce a liquid gruel at a lower dilution. The child would then not have to drink so much to get the same energy intake.

In some places, like Northern Uganda, this is already done. Here a groundnut and sesame seed paste, which is rich in fat, is added to the traditional weaning diet. Unfortunately this solution is not always as easy as it sounds. Foods with fat may not be locally available, or they may be too expensive. Even where they can be brought in, changing food habits is never an easy task.

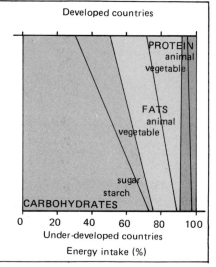

Figure 3.10
Differences in the composition of the diet in developed and under-developed countries.

CHAPTER 4
Why eat?

4.1
WHAT MAKES YOU WANT TO EAT?

Q 1
How do you know when you want something to eat? Write down four or
five words or phrases which explain your feelings.

Most answers to question 1 will contain the word 'hungry'.

Q 2
How are you feeling now — very hungry, fairly hungry, or not hungry at all?

Your answer will probably depend on how long it is since your
last meal or snack, and not on whether your body is in urgent
need of food. Look at the people in figure 4.1. They would
probably answer 'very hungry' or 'fairly hungry' to question 2.
Both look healthy; they are not suffering like people who are
seriously short of food. Their feelings, and yours, are just useful
reminders to eat regularly. Another word for what we feel is
appetite, defined in the dictionary as 'the desire to eat'.

Appetites can be increased and reduced. Look at the pictures
in figure 4.2. Imagine how you would feel in each situation.

Q 3
Which situations would increase your appetite and which reduce it? Write
your answers in a table and add examples from your own experience.

Figure 4.1

Figure 4.2

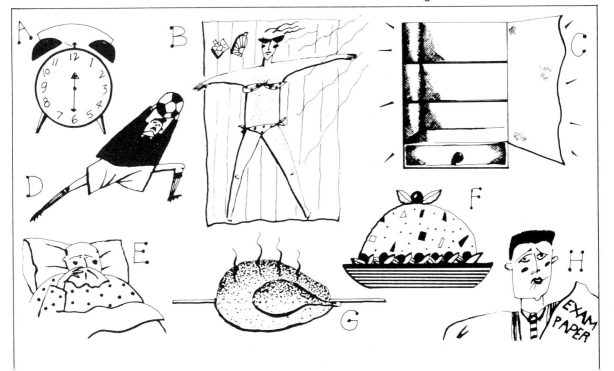

These situations are worth discussing in class. Appetite control is complicated; learning about it could help you to stick to a good diet. Habits plays a large part in appetite control. Many people become hungry around their usual meal times, although we are not always able to eat when we would wish.

Q 4

What happens to your appetite when you miss a meal?

Q 5

Most people come to no harm by occasionally missing meals. What do you think would happen to the appetite if meals were often missed, or only taken irregularly?

Are you always hungry before you start to eat a meal or snack? The answer is probably 'no'. Often snacks are eaten just because we enjoy eating. A meal can be a social occasion, a time for being with friends and not just for satisfying hunger. Do you always stop eating when you no longer feel hungry? Again the answer is likely to be 'no'. Often we over-eat on special occasions.

Q 6

In what circumstances are you likely to start eating without feeling hungry or to go on eating after your appetite is satisfied? Make your own list. How could such a list help in appetite control?

Appetite is a body mechanism intended to prompt us to eat enough food at regular intervals. It should tell us when to start and when to stop — if we take trouble to train it.

Figure 4.3
A meal can be a social occasion.

Figure 4.5

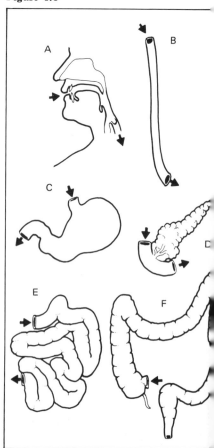

4.2
WHAT FOLLOWS EATING?

Food cannot be used by the body unless it is digested. Indigestion might have been in your list headed 'decreases appetite'. Fortunately our bodies are very good at digesting food. We don't usually think about digestion at all unless we get signals that something is wrong. Vomiting and diarrhoea are unpleasant but useful ways for normally healthy adults to get rid of irritating material as quickly as possible. Indigestion pains could be serious, but most are due to 'uncomfortable digestion' rather than 'incomplete digestion'. Foods which are thought to cause indigestion include those which remain longest in the stomach.

Many strong flavouring substances in food are volatile and can return to the mouth. Any unpleasant feeling will be linked with foods being tasted for a second time. Food which looks, smells, and tastes appetizing causes digestive juices to flow readily from the salivary glands. So, digestion gets off to a better start with attractive food than with unattractive food. Even so, very nearly all food which is eaten is completely digested.

What makes digestion so efficient? Obviously the digestive system must be well-designed for the job. Look at worksheet NM4. It shows the *alimentary canal*, known as the *gut*. You can think of this as a continuous tube with food entering at one end

Figure 4.4
Onions have a strong flavour.
Digestion gets off to a good start
with pleasant flavours.

Figure 4.6

NO NEED FOR HIS
FOOD TO BE PUT
THROUGH A
FOOD PROCESSOR

Figure 4.7
Food in the gut is churned and
pushed along by contractions in both
these muscle layers.

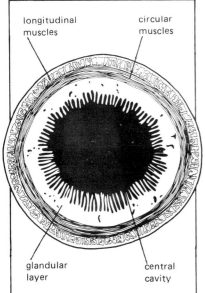

longitudinal
muscles

circular
muscles

glandular
layer

central
cavity

(the mouth) and faeces leaving at the other end (the anus). The walls of this tube are muscular and lined with cells which produce slimy mucus to lubricate it. Figure 4.8 shows an enlarged diagram of a section through the gut wall.

The gut varies along its length according to the digestive changes taking place within it. Some parts of the gut receive secretions from glands. Figure 4.5 divides the gut into its functional parts. Compare it with the diagram on worksheet NM4 and use the information there to answer question 7.

Q 7
For each of the six parts of the gut state:
a its name
b the effect on food of muscular action
c the name(s) of any glands which secrete into it
d the name(s) of digestive secretions active within it
e any chemical changes which take place within it.

4.3
WHAT NEEDS DIGESTING, AND WHY?
The nutrients which have to be digested are starches, proteins, fats, and the sugars known as sucrose, lactose, and maltose. All are molecules too big to pass through the cell membranes of the lining of the gut and the walls of the blood vessels. Unless these molecules are made smaller by digestion, they cannot be carried by blood to the parts of the body which need them.

Q 8
a Name the substances formed by complete digestion of: starches; proteins; fats; maltose?
b What can be said about all these products of digestion?

Q 9
Glucose, vitamin C, the B vitamins, alcohol, water, and salt are all substances in food which need no digestion. What does this tell you about them?

Changing a meal made up of solid pieces of food and liquids into a watery pulp can be done by crushing and mixing. This begins in the mouth and goes on in the stomach and small intestine. The result is much the same as if the meal had been put in a liquidizer. Soluble substances dissolve and insoluble substances are broken into pieces small enough to be suspended.

Bile secreted by the liver emulsifies fat so that it remains well-mixed with the watery pulp. Dissolving, suspending, and emulsifying are all physical processes. They do not alter the *size* of molecules — only chemical changes can do that.

Enzymes are needed to make chemical changes to food in the gut. Each chemical change requires its own particular type of enzyme. (See worksheet FSM 8 Enzymes.)

Q 10
Using worksheet NM4, name the enzymes involved in the complete digestion of: starches; proteins; fats; maltose.

4.4

WHAT HELPS ENZYME ACTIVITY?
What is the effect of salivary amylase on starch?

||| YOU WILL NEED: ||||||||||||||||||||||||||||||||||||||||||||||||||||||||||||||||||||||||||||||||

1 % starch solution   Clock or stopwatch
Saliva solution   Cup
Clean water   Beaker
Iodine papers   Stirring rod

5-ml (tea) spoon
Test-tube

1 Make a solution of your saliva. First rinse your mouth out with clean water. Then hold some clean water in your mouth for about half a minute, moving it around with your tongue, before collecting it in a beaker.

2 Measure 5 ml starch solution into the test-tube. Use the stirring rod to put a drop of the solution onto an iodine paper. Note the colour change.

3 Add 5 ml saliva solution to the test-tube and stir the mixture.

4 Put a drop of the starch and saliva mixture onto another strip of iodine paper. Look for a colour change.

5 Repeat instruction 4 at 30-second intervals until no further colour change is seen. Keep the test-tube warm throughout by holding your hand around it. Keep the contents thoroughly mixed using the stirring rod.

Q 11
a What colour change indicates that starch is present?
b What time was needed for the amylase to complete its action on the starch?
c Why were you advised to keep the mixture warm and well-mixed?

Q 12
Which of the following is the correct interpretation of the evidence from this experiment? Amylase changes starch into: a colourless compound; maltose; a different substance.

What is the effect of the size of food particles on the way trypsin works?

||| YOU WILL NEED: ||||||||||||||||||||||||||||||||||||||||||||||||||||||||||||||||||||||||||||||||||||||||||||||||

2 equal-sized cubes of cooked   2 test-tubes
egg white (0.5-cm cubes)   Nylon sieve
Trypsin solution   Beaker and insulating material
Sodium bicarbonate solution   Thermometer, −10 °C to 110 °C
Warm water   5-ml (tea)spoon
Labels   Stirring rod

1 Label the test-tubes A and B and into each put 5 ml trypsin solution and 5 ml sodium bicarbonate solution.

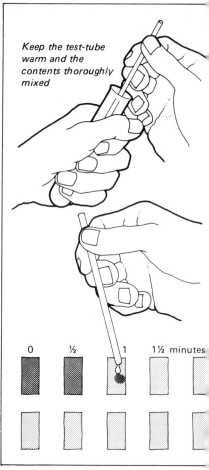

Keep the test-tube warm and the contents thoroughly mixed

0   ½   1   1½ minutes

Figure 4.8

Figure 4.9

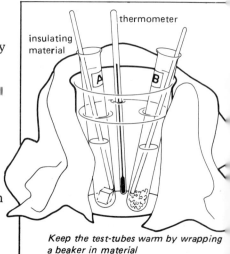

thermometer

insulating material

A   B

Keep the test-tubes warm by wrapping a beaker in material

2 Put one whole cube of egg white into test-tube A. Sieve the second cube of egg white and add it to test-tube B. Stir both test-tubes gently to mix their contents.

3 Put the test-tubes into a beaker of water at 40 °C for 30 minutes. Insulating material wrapped around the beaker will keep the water warm (see figure 4.9).

4 At intervals, remove both test-tubes from the beaker, rock them gently to mix their contents and look for evidence of enzyme action. The insoluble protein material (the cooked egg white) becomes soluble, less solid is seen, and the surrounding liquid becomes cloudy. Eventually all the solid will disappear.

Q 13
How does particle size affect the action of trypsin on cooked egg white?

Q 14
Assuming that what you have found out about trypsin applies to other digestive enzymes, give a reason why emulsification of fat by bile is such an important part of digestion.

The evidence gained from the two experiments in this section should help you to answer the next three questions.

Q 15
How important do you think the mouth is in the process of digestion?

Q 16
Why is the stomach shaped like a bag and not a tube like the rest of the gut?

Q 17
How does the length of the small intestine (about 7 m) help in digestion?

4.5
HOW DO NUTRIENTS GET INTO THE BLOOD?
The process of materials passing through the wall of the gut and into the blood is called *absorption*. This occurs mainly in the small intestine (although alcohol and some water are absorbed from the stomach, and water is also absorbed from the colon, together with vitamins B_{12} and K).

The small intestine has a fairly small diameter (about 2.25 cm) but a great length (about 7 m) and an enormous internal surface area (probably more than 300 m²). Figure 4.11 shows the lining folded and covered with minute projections, called *villi* (singular *villus*). Each villus is only one millimetre long. Figure 4.12 is a photograph of villi, greatly magnified. Notice the close packing of the villi and their uneven surfaces. This creates the enormous surface in contact with the food being digested.

Digestion produces food particles which can pass into the cells lining the small intestine. Particles present in high concentration simply diffuse in, but other nutrients are drawn in by an active process. The minerals iron and calcium are actively absorbed when the body needs them. (See Chapters 10 and 11.)

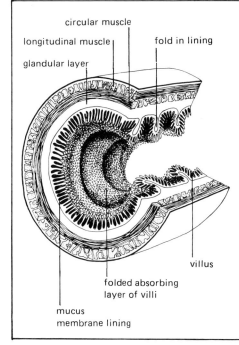

circular muscle
longitudinal muscle
fold in lining
glandular layer
villus
folded absorbing layer of villi
mucus membrane lining

Figure 4.10
Transverse and longitudinal sections through the small intestine wall.

Figure 4.11
Photograph of villi, greatly magnified.

Within the walls of the small intestine, digestion of sugars and protein fragments is completed. Water-soluble materials pass straight into the blood. Emulsified fatty materials pass into another body fluid (*lymph*) before entering the blood.

Q 18
Which nutrient materials pass straight into blood and which into lymph first? (Don't forget about the vitamins.)

Non-nutrient materials taken in by the mouth are also absorbed. These include drugs and food additives.

Q 19
a Where is alcohol absorbed?
b Why is the effect of alcohol felt more quickly when taken before a meal?

4.6
WHAT HAPPENS TO THE INDIGESTIBLE PARTS OF FOOD?

The processes of digestion and absorption are very efficient. The only materials which reach the end of the small intestine and enter the colon in any quantity are water and the fibrous tissues in plant foods. These are made up of large-molecule substances, mainly cellulose, pectin, and lignin. They cannot be digested in the human gut, but they play an important part in the efficient working of the digestive system.

Figure 4.12 *(above)*
Priston Mill near Bath. The grinding stones are encased in wood. Grain in sacks is fed to the stones from the hopper.

What is dietary fibre like? Can it be detected in foods? Examine some samples of its main constituents.

IIII YOU WILL NEED: IIIIIIIIIIIIIIIIIIIIIIIIIIIIIIIIIIIIIIIIIIIIIIIIIIIIIIIIIIIIIIIIIIIIIIIIIIIIIIIIIIIIIIIIIIIIIIIIIIII

Small quantites of cellulose, pectin,   4 small dishes
ligin, and wheat bran   Stirring rod
Water

1 Note down the appearance and texture of cellulose, pectin, and lignin.

2 Add a little water to each and stir. Describe the results. (Use words such as gelatinous, gummy, absorbent, granular.)

3 Examine the bran. Note any resemblances to and differences from the dietary fibre constituents. Add water and compare the results with the results from instruction 2.

Q 20
Would you always be able to detect the presence of dietary fibre in a food? (*Note.* Lignin only occurs in plant tissues which are recognizably woody.)

The strong attraction which dietary fibre has for water determines the bulk and consistency of the faeces. Investigate the water-binding capacity of the cellulose used in coldwater paste.

IIII YOU WILL NEED: IIIIIIIIIIIIIIIIIIIIIIIIIIIIIIIIIIIIIIIIIIIIIIIIIIIIIIIIIIIIIIIIIIIIIIIIIIIIIIIIIIIIIIIIIIIIIIIIIIII

10 g cellulosic wallpaper paste   Basin or beaker
(2 rounded 5-ml (tea) spoonfuls)   Spoon for stirring
250 ml water in a graduated cylinder

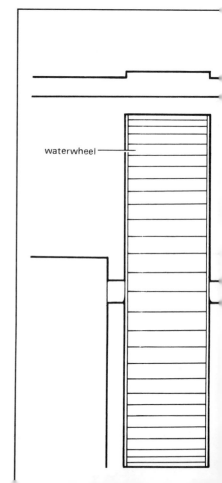
waterwheel

1 Add 100 ml water from the graduated cylinder to the 10 g cellulose granules in a beaker or basin. Stir and leave for a few minutes.

2 Add more water, a little at a time, from the cylinder while stirring. Continue until you have a gelatinous semi-solid mixture.

3 Estimate the mass of water that can be bound by 1 g cellulose.

To remain healthy, there should be sufficient dietary fibre to hold enough water to keep the faeces soft and bulky. Otherwise water is absorbed through the wall of the colon leaving small hard faeces which are slow-moving and difficult to pass.

Dietary fibre molecules bind other molecules as well as water and remove them from the body in the faeces. Some useful mineral matter in food is lost this way. Isn't this a waste? Possibly, but it is also a safeguard against excessive amounts of minerals getting into the body. Other materials are removed by fibre which, if allowed to remain in the colon, would break down into poisonous substances.

Figure 4.13 *(below)*
The mill mechanism. The power to turn the stones comes entirely from water flowing past the water wheel.

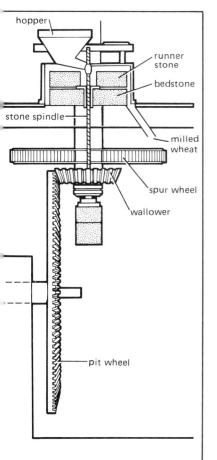

BACKGROUND READING

THE FIBRE STORY
Over the last twenty years sales in Britain of wholemeal bread, which is high in fibre, have almost doubled even though total bread sales have dropped. Why the sudden interest in high-fibre foods? Fibre used to be considered an unimportant part of the diet. Since about 1970, it has become a significant sales-boosting feature and many best-selling books have been written about it. The reason, quite simply, is that more people are starting to believe not only that fibre is good for you, but that too little actually does you harm.

The experts now believe that fibre is needed to stop the bowel defects that cause constipation and diverticulitis. These conditions are common in countries where little fibre is eaten, and uncommon where diets include lots of vegetables and unrefined cereals. The medical treatment is to get patients to eat wholemeal bread or take spoonfuls of bran with meals.

The arguments for a high-fibre diet seem pretty good. Switching from white bread (2.7 per cent fibre) to wholemeal bread (8.5 per cent fibre) would certainly give us more of the fibre we need. However, changing people's dietary habits is not easy. There may be problems in getting the bread industry to start mass producing wholemeal loaves. Millers would no longer be able to sell the bran as animal food and the many bakeries geared to to producing white bread would have to make changes. Furthermore, as people can't eat as much wholemeal bread as white bread (because it's more filling), the bread industry might lose sales.

CHAPTER 5
Why drink?

5.1
WHAT MAKES YOU WANT TO DRINK?

Q 1
Each person in figure 5.1 wants a drink. How do they know?
Describe their feelings.

Q 2
a What do you think causes their sensations of thirst?
b What would quench their thirsts?

Your answers to question 2 probably give two different causes
for the same effect — thirst — and only one cure. Why is this?
Try to obtain some scientific evidence about causing and
quenching thirst.

Carry out a class investigation into the effects of different drinks
on feelings of thirst.

|||| YOU WILL NEED: |||||||||||||||||||||||||||||||||||||||||||||||||||||||||||||||||||||
Drinking water   Cup or mug for each member of
Salted drinking water   of the class
                               500-ml measuring jug
                               15-ml (table)spoon

1 Record your present feelings as 'very thirsty', 'a bit thirsty',
or 'not thirsty'.

Figure 5.1
Sensations of thirst:
a *marathon runner* b *sunbathing* c *eating crisps.*

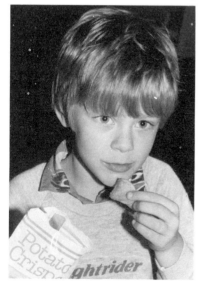

Figure 5.3

2 Divide yourselves into three groups, approximately equal in numbers, according to alphabetical order.

3 Each member of the class will have a drink, as follows:

Group A   200 ml water
Group B   200 ml salted water
Group C   15 ml water

4 After about 30 minutes (at a convenient point in the lesson) record your thirst sensations again and note whether they have changed since you had the drink.

5 Find out how many in your group now feel 'more thirsty', 'less thirsty', or 'about the same'.

Put your results into percentages of the number in your group.

6 Display results for the whole class, filling in a table like figure 5.2 on the blackboard.

	More thirsty		Less thirsty		About the same	
	number	%	number	%	number	%
Group A (number =)						
Group B (number =)						
Group C (number =)						

Figure 5.2

Q 3
a Those members of the class who are thirsty should now have a drink. Which should they choose: 200 ml water, 200 ml salted water, or 15 ml water?
b
b Do the results of the class investigation agree with your decision?

5.2
WHY IS THERE SO MUCH WATER IN THE BODY?
Water forms a large part of our bodies — about sixty percent by weight.

Q 4
a What, approximately, is the weight of water in the body of a 70 kg man?
b How much is this in litres?

Water transports nutrients
Water has many functions in the body. The one most obviously linked to nutrition is the transport of nutrients to all parts of the body. Water-soluble nutrients are carried in solution in the water of the blood. Fatty nutrients are carried in blood in the form of an emulsion.

Q 5
Name *four* nutrients which are present in the water part of blood.

Q 6

Name *two* nutrients which are in blood as an emulsion.

Q 7

What is the difference between a solution and an emulsion?

Fatty nutrients in blood are linked to special proteins which help to keep them emulsified. This is similar to the way butter fat is kept mixed with the water in milk. Other proteins in blood link to mineral elements such as iron and calcium to help move them around the body. (See Chapters 10 and 11.)

Nutrients pass out of blood into cells which need them. Dissolved and emulsified nutrient particles have to be small enough to pass through cell membranes.

Q 8

What are the substances entering cells which come from the following food components:
a proteins
b starches
c fats?

Water transports unwanted materials

The second important function of water in blood is the transport of unwanted materials to the kidneys for removal from the body. Unwanted materials include *urea* (a waste product made from amino acids not needed by cells for making new proteins) and salt and other water-soluble substances absorbed from food in excessive amounts. All these unwanted substances are removed from the body in urine, the watery solution made by the kidneys (see figure 5.4.)

Q 9

What will happen to any vitamin C absorbed in greater amounts than can be held by the tissues of the body?

Q 10

a What type of nutrients cannot be got rid of in urine when too much has been absorbed?
b Why is this?

5.3
HOW MUCH DO WE NEED TO DRINK EACH DAY?

On average, between 1 litre and 2.5 litres of water pass out of the body each day as urine. Some water is also removed with faeces. In addition, at least 1 litre of water is lost from the body each day in breath and sweat. Try this simple test which shows that your body is giving off water vapour all the time.

‖‖ YOU WILL NEED: ‖‖

4 strips of cobalt chloride test paper

Wire rack (cake cooling rack)
Access to a warm oven

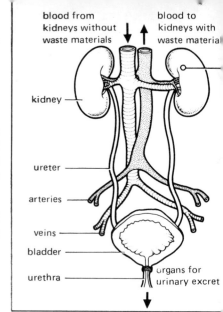

Figure 5.4
The human kidney system.

Figure 5.5

Watch the blue colour of the cobalt chloride paper develop

Figure 5.7

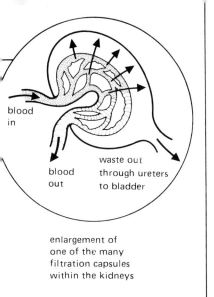

blood in

blood out

waste out through ureters to bladder

enlargement of one of the many filtration capsules within the kidneys

Figure 5.6
Breathe out three or four times.

1 Put the test papers on the wire rack in a warm oven (figure 5.5). Leave the door open. Watch the blue colour of the cobalt chloride paper develop. It is only blue when completely dry. In the presence of water it turns to a very pale pink.

2 Remove two strips of cobalt chloride paper from the oven. Leave one exposed to the air in the room. Hold the other strip close to your mouth as you breathe out three or four times. Do not of course put it into your mouth.

3 Compare the colours of the two strips. Record which strip showed less blue colour.

4 Remove two more strips from the oven. Leave one exposed to the air as before, and hold the other between your cupped hands for 2 minutes.

5 Compare the colours of the strips. Record which strip showed less blue colour.

Q 11
What did your results tell you about water vapour in:
a breath
b air close to the skin
c normal air?

What does this tell us about water losses from the body? Each day we need to drink enough water to replace all losses of water in urine, faeces, breath, and sweat.

Q 12
From the information given at the beginning of this section, what do you estimate is the minimum amount of water you should be drinking every day?

Q 13
In what circumstances would you expect to drink well above this minimum? Give *two* examples and an explanation for each.

Drinking more water than the body needs is not a problem. The kidneys simply make more watery urine.

5.4
WHAT HAPPENS IF YOU CAN'T GET ENOUGH TO DRINK?
Thirst is a signal from the brain that the blood has become too salty and that more water is needed to dilute it. We respond by making every effort to obtain a drink of water — either plain or flavoured. But what if there is no water to drink?

Q 14
a Why is the shipwrecked sailor just as badly off as the stranded desert traveller in figure 5.7?
b What would a drink of sea water do to the saltinesss of the sailor's blood?
c Do the results of your investigation in section 5.1 into the effects of different drinks on thirst agree with your opinion? If not, try to find an explanation.

Figure 5.8
Marathon runner cooling off.

Figure 5.9
Hot and sweaty work.

Figure 5.10

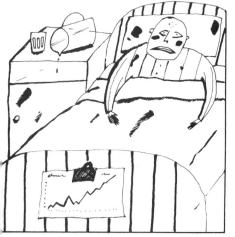

Lack of water to drink is more harmful than shortage of food. It is possible to survive for several weeks without food, but only a few days without water. The body can protect itself, to some extent, against shortage of water by reducing its water output. It can't stop losses due to breathing and sweating, but it can limit the production of urine. The special brain cells which detect increased saltiness of blood cause a *hormone* (a chemical messenger) to be sent to the kidneys with the message 'Cut down the amount of water leaving the body in urine'. This helps, but there must always be some water lost in urine. The amount depends on how much urea has got to be dissolved to get it out of the body.

Q 15
How would the amount of protein in the diet affect the amount of urine which has got to be produced each day?

5.5
DEHYDRATION — WHAT IS IT AND WHO IS AT RISK?
Dehydration means removal of water. The medical condition known as dehydration occurs when more water is being lost from the body than is being replaced by drinking. Thirst protects most people much of the time, but there are circumstances in which it is ineffective.

Q 16
The runner in figure 5.8 is sweating heavily but does not feel particularly thirsty. Why is this? (*Clue*: Sweat contains salt as well as water.)

Q 17
The worker in figure 5.9 is beginning to feel heat-fatigue and soon he will be given some salted water. Why should he drink it even if he does not feel thirsty? Why is salted water better for him than plain?

Q 18
The patient in figure 5.10 has a high temperature and needs plenty of water to replace that lost through sweating. What other symptoms could cause the body to lose large amounts of water?

Seriously ill patients may be too weak to help themselves to a drink or even ask for one. Elderly patients sometimes try not to drink too much because of incontinence. *All* patients should be encouraged to drink freely. Otherwise there is a risk of dehydration.

If only a crying baby could tell us what is wrong! It could be pain or hunger, but it is likely to be thirst. A baby's body contains a higher percentage of water than an adult's. Babies lose water very readily by sweating. Any sickness, diarrhoea, or high temperature can reduce the water in a baby's body to a dangerous level. A baby can quickly become ill through dehydration.

Q 19
Should a baby who is ill with a fever or tummy upset be given something to drink apart from milk? If so, what?

Babies in poor countries where food is scarce, and the risk of infection is high, frequently suffer from diarrhoea and this brings dehydration. The World Health Organization sees this as one of the greatest problems it faces. Much more knowledge of the condition and how it can be recognized and treated is needed. Worksheet NM9 gives more details of the problem of dehydration and illustrates some short and long term solutions to it.

5.6
FOOD AND DRINK FOR BABIES: WHY IS BREAST MILK BEST?

A baby growing inside the womb gets all its supplies from the mother's blood.

Once the baby is born it has to get its nutrients in another way. The mother's breasts make milk to feed the baby. Babies who are breast-fed need no other form of food for the first four months at least. Breast-fed babies form a strong attachment to their mothers. Breast-feeding can be a very satisfying experience for the mother.

The content of human breast milk adapts to the baby's needs for both food and drink. As a baby begins each feed, the milk which comes from the breast is very watery, quenching the baby's thirst. Later on it becomes more concentrated, supplying the baby with food. Changing to the second breast gives the baby another watery drink. This change in taste seems to help the baby decide whether he or she has had enough. Milk from a bottle cannot vary in composition like this. Bottle-fed babies should be offered water to drink as well as milk.

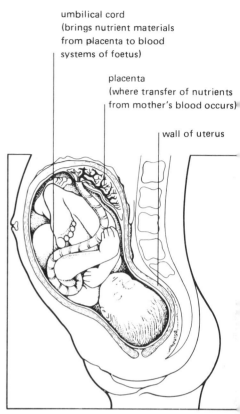

umbilical cord
(brings nutrient materials from placenta to blood systems of foetus)

placenta
(where transfer of nutrients from mother's blood occurs)

wall of uterus

Figure 5.12
Baby inside the womb.

Figure 5.13
Breast-feeding.

Figure 5.11
Is it pain, hunger, or thirst?

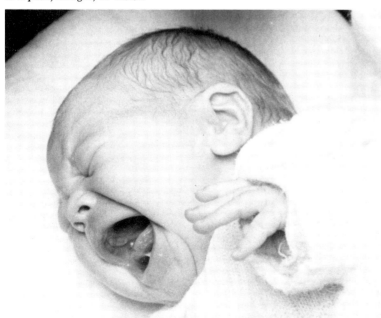

The composition of human breast milk is exactly right for human babies. All mammals provide milk which is right for their own young — but not for others. Different types of infant mammals have different needs. Look at worksheet NM10 which shows the composition of milk from several different mammals.

Q 20
Name *two* (or if possible three) types of mammal whose milk is used for human food in the United Kingdom.

It is safe for children and adults to drink milk from other mammals (as long as it is clean), but such milk will not be right for babies. When a baby has to be bottle-fed, a special milk feed has to be used which copies the composition of human milk as closely as possible. The powder (often called 'infant formula') is made using dried cow's milk and other additives. Look at the average compositions of human milk, cow's milk, and infant formula made into a liquid feed shown on worksheet NM11.

If the infant formula is made up carefully (according to instructions on the packet), and given to the baby in a perfectly clean, sterilized bottle, there is a good chance that the baby will thrive. Certainly this method of feeding has proved of great benefit when breast-feeding has not been possible.

Q 21
Very few mothers are unable to breast-feed, but some find it difficult. Suggest some circumstances which could make breast-feeding difficult.

Before deciding to change from breast-feeding to bottle-feeding, a mother should remember the following six points.

Figure 5.14
Bottle feeding a baby.

Figure 5.15
Instructions for bottle feeding.

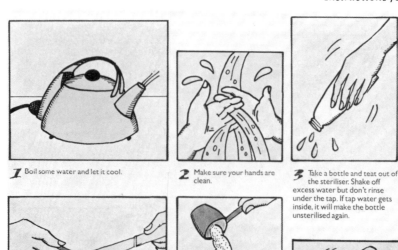

1 Boil some water and let it cool.

2 Make sure your hands are clean.

3 Take a bottle and teat out of the steriliser. Shake off excess water but don't rinse under the tap. If tap water gets inside, it will make the bottle unsterilised again.

4 Using the measuring marks on the side of the bottle, fill the bottle with the right amount of water. Use the boiled water that you left to cool.

5 Measure the exact amount of powder, using the special scoop provided with the milk. Level the powder in the scoop using a knife. Don't pack the powder down tight.

6 Add the powder to the water in the bottle.

7 Screw on the cap and shake the bottle well.

Figure 5.16
Mammals suckling young:
a *sheep* b *pig* c *cow.*

Figure 5.17

1 Mistakes can be made when mixing the powdered milk. Too dilute a mixture will not give all the nutrients the baby needs. Too concentrated a mixture will make the baby thirsty.

2 Bottle-fed babies sometimes overfeed and become fat.

3 Infection can occur if bottles are not properly sterilized or if the infant formula is mixed with impure water. Most Western countries can rely on a clean water supply. In poor countries water is one of the main sources of infection, causing serious symptoms of fever and diarrhoea in babies.

4 Breast milk contains antibodies which have developed in the mother's blood. These give the baby immunity to some infectious diseases. Bottle-fed babies do not have this protection.

5 Bottle-feeding costs more than breast-feeding.

6 During pregnancy, a mother lays down extra fat stores in her body to be used for milk production after the baby is born. Breast-feeding uses up these fat stores and this helps her regain her figure.

5.7
WHAT ABOUT SALT INTAKES?
The thirst control mechanism is linked to the concentration of sodium in the blood. So is the production of urine. Most of the sodium in our bodies comes from the salt in our food and salt should be considered an essential nutrient in our diets. Salt occurs naturally in most foods. Animal foods are higher in salt than plant foods.

With very few exceptions, normal diets provide more than enough salt and the excess has to be removed in urine. Most of us can do this quite easily, but babies cannot. The water lost in urine removing this extra salt could bring about dehydration. Salt *must not* be added to baby foods.

Q 22
Which *two* kinds of people (noted in section 5.5) need extra supplies of salt?

Q 23
What are the main sources of salt in your diet? (See Chapter 3.)

Q 24
Why is salt added by manufacturers to so many processed foods?

People with high blood pressure (*hypertension*) are more likely to suffer from heart disease and strokes than those with normal blood pressure. Although there is no proof that high salt intakes *cause* high blood pressure, a lot of people with high blood pressure have been found to be taking a lot of salt in their diets. Because of this, reduction in the average consumption of salt by the people in this country is one of the dietary guidelines for better health (see Chapters 2, 3, and 15).

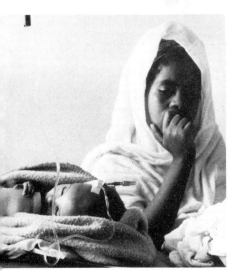

Figure 5.18
An Ethiopian mother watches as her baby recieves rehydration treatment after severe diarrhoea brought on by bottle-feeding.

Figure 5.19
Poster used in the Philippines to encourage breast-feeding.

Figure 5.20
A dirty feeding bottle.

Q 25
What difficulties might an adult have in putting the dietary guideline to reduce salt intakes into practice?

Q 26
What advantage would there be in delaying as long as possible the addition of salt to the food of a toddler?

BACKGROUND READING

BREAST IS BEST
In spite of all the advantages of breast feeding, many mothers look for other ways to feed their young. Attitudes to breast feeding depend upon culture, social class, and education. For example, in 1500 B.C. Egyptian women of high status would give their babies to 'wet nurses' to suckle. They felt that breast feeding was beneath them. This practice became very popular amongst the upper classes of Europe, reaching a peak in the eighteenth century. Many babies were actually farmed out to poor women where the conditions of poverty meant that a large number died. In 1748 one observer wrote of wet nurses, 'the ancient custom of exposing children to wild beasts or drowning was quicker and more humane'. Wet nursing died out in England shortly after the production of the first powdered milk in 1866.

Advertising can also shape attitudes towards breast feeding. In developing countries powdered milk manufacturers spend millions of pounds advertising their products on radio and T.V. It is now widely believed that bottle feeding in these countries is a cause of malnutrition and disease. Mothers are also visited by company nurses in baby clinics and maternity wards. These nurses give out free milk samples and try very hard to persuade mothers to use powdered milk.

Doctors, nurses, and hospital staff also fall victim to company pressure. They often get visits from company sales staff who hand out free gifts like holidays, theatre tickets, and hospital equipment. In return, the medical staff must promise to use and promote the company's brand of powdered milk. One hospital administrator in the Philippines said that he could have anything he asked for.

Some mothers are unaware of the advantages to their health if they breast feed their babies. Contrary to some opinions, breasts are not mis-shapen by breast feeding. These days bras give the necessary support. Another advantage is that mothers who breast feed are less likely to be overweight. A good diet ensures the health of the mother and a good supply of milk for the baby. Current child-care guidance encourages mothers to breast feed their babies for the well-being of both.

Although many doctors in developing countries are now aware of the dangers of powdered milk, they also know how hard it is to change attitudes. They feel that no matter what they do or say, the companies will always have enough money to make sure that they win the war of words.

CHAPTER 6
Using food energy

6.1
WHAT DOES THE BODY NEED FROM FOOD?
Living cells use food for the two purposes shown in figure 6.1.

Figure 6.1

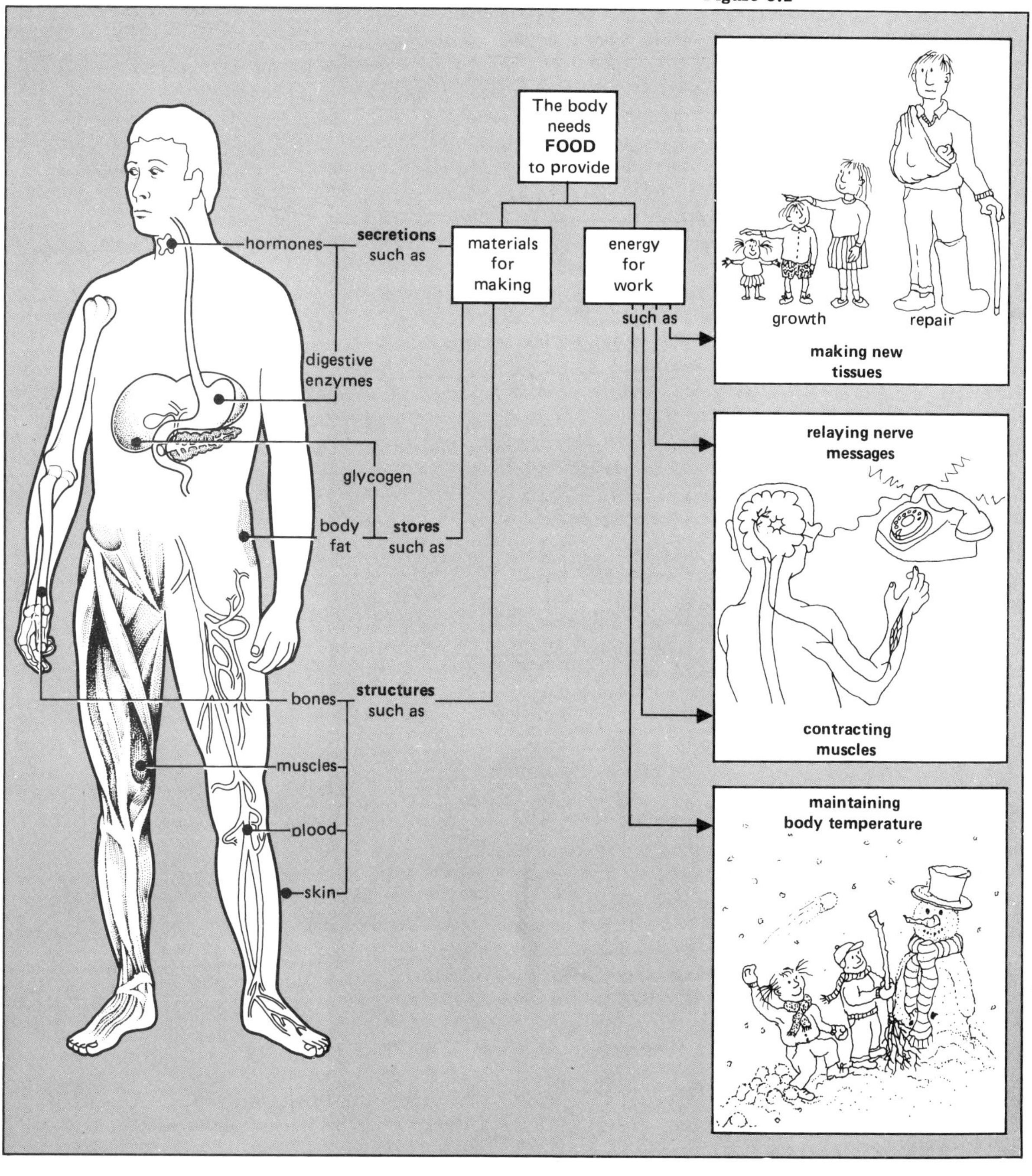

The body needs **FOOD** to provide

materials for making — secretions such as — hormones — digestive enzymes

stores such as — glycogen — body fat

structures such as — bones — muscles — blood — skin

energy for work such as

making new tissues — growth — repair

relaying nerve messages

contracting muscles

maintaining body temperature

Energy will be considered first because the body puts energy first. When the body is short of food, it will use everything available to supply its needs for energy — even the nutrients which ought to be used for making body structures.

6.2
WHAT IS ENERGY AND HOW IS IT MEASURED?
When you read 'Food has energy' you should not think of the energy as something that can be extracted, like fats, sugars, salts, dietary fibre, or water. It is just a way of describing what the food is capable of doing. In much the same way, if you say someone has good health, it does not mean that you could extract the health. It means that because they have it they are able to do things which could not be done without it.

Energy is not easy to describe. It is needed to heat things up, to make things move, or to send an electric current through a circuit. In fact, for any useful job a source of energy is needed. (This is why one definition of energy is 'the capacity for doing work'.) Energy is not actually used up in doing any of these jobs. In this respect it is rather like money. When you buy a bus ticket, it may seem to you that the money has gone for good, but it has really only changed hands. Scientists have proposed a law which expresses this idea: it is called the Law of Conservation of Energy. This can be expressed briefly as 'energy cannot be created or destroyed'.

This means that when we want some work done, we first have to find a source of energy. When we 'use' energy to do the work, we are simply transferring it somewhere else — making it 'change hands' like the money for the bus ticket.

Q 1
What is the main source of energy used for:
a heating your school
b driving a car
c growing plants?

Q 2
What energy sources are used for generating electricity in Britain?

We can often tell very easily when energy is being transferred because we can detect the transfer with our senses. If a light is switched on we can see it, we can hear a radio, and we can warm our hands in front of a fire. In these examples our bodies are at the receiving end of the transfer. Sometimes it is obvious that a transfer of energy is occurring because the effects are visible — wheels turn, or a bomb explodes. But there are plenty of cases where the transfer is not obvious: we cannot always tell when an electric current is flowing, or when a chemical action is taking place.

Energy is sometimes labelled according to the job being done: heat energy, light energy, moving (or mechanical) energy, and so on. (We often label money in the same way — bus money,

Figure 6.2

dinner money, holiday money — according to how it is being used.) At other times, it is useful to label energy according to its source. If it is stored in a battery, it might be called battery energy, though it is more usually called chemical energy. Food and fuels are also said to have chemical energy, as the chemicals in them are reorganized when the energy is transferred.

Q 3
How would you label the energy when it is used in
a making new tissues
b relaying nerve messages
c contracting muscles
d maintaining body temperatures?

Energy must be measured — if only so that it can be priced for selling. Measuring energy involves using it to do work, then measuring the work done. People using energy for different kinds of jobs have invented their own way of measuring the work done, just as people in different countries invented their own ways of measuring length. When talking about the electricity supply, the unit was the kilowatt hour (kWh). This is the energy transferred when an appliance rated at 1000 watts (1 kW) is used for an hour.

For *heating* small quantities, especially in chemistry, the calorie was used. This is the energy needed to raise the temperature of 1 g water by 1° C. You still find the much larger 'British Thermal Unit' used in connection with the supply of large amounts of heat.

In *mechanical* work the joule is the unit used. This is the energy needed to lift a weight of 1 newton (equivalent to a mass of about 100 g) vertically upwards through a height of 1 m.

Calories, kilowatt hours, and joules are all used for measuring energy transfer. Don't get confused. Changing from one to another is just a matter of arithmetic. Fortunately, nowadays most people have agreed to use the same unit, the joule, which makes comparison much easier.

Useful conversion factors
A 'food Calorie' is worth 1000 ordinary calories and so should strictly be called a kilocalorie.

A calorie is worth 4.2 joules (and so, of course, a kilocalorie is worth 4.2 kilojoules).

An appliance rated at 1000 watts (1 kW) will transfer energy at the rate of a kilojoule every second, so a kilowatt hour of energy is worth 60×60 kilojoules.

Q 4
Which is the smallest of these energy units: a kilowatt hour, a joule, a calorie?

Q 5
What do the prefixes 'kilo' and 'mega' stand for?

Q 6
The energy value of a small piece of Victoria sponge cake is given as
115 kcal on worksheet M21.
a What is this in kilojoules (kJ)?
b Does your answer agree with the figure for kJ on worksheet M21? Why
do you think this is?

6.3
HOW DO WE GET THE KIND OF ENERGY WE NEED?
The most useful sources of energy are those in which it can be
conveniently stored and easily released to do the kind of work
we want. A dry cell (battery) is a convenient store of energy for
working a torch or radio. A stretched elastic band is a useful
store of energy for anyone using a catapult! Car engines are
designed to transfer the chemical energy stored in petrol to
movement (or kinetic) energy.

Many foods are useful sources of energy, but you cannot tell
just by looking which are the important energy stores. Try this
experiment on two similar looking foods.

||||| YOU WILL NEED: |||||||||||||||||||||||||||||||||||||||||||||||||||||||||||||||||||||||||||||||||||||||||||
5 g glucose (half a 5-ml (tea) spoon)
5 g salt (half a 5-ml (tea) spoon)

Tin lid
Source of heat (Bunsen burner and tripod, or hot plate of cooker)
Tongs

1 Put the glucose and salt in separate piles on the tin lid. Make
sure you know which is which.

2 Using the tongs, carefully put the lid over a strong source of
heat. Make sure that the two substances are heated equally.
Continue heating until no further change occurs. ⚠

Q 7
From which food was a store of chemical energy transferred?

Q 8
What word could be used to describe the transfer mechanism?

Q 9
What happened to the food when its energy had gone?

Q 10
Why would this method of energy transfer be unsuitable for use by the body?

Q 11
a Why do an electric lamp and a car engine get hot when switched on?
b Do you think this always happens when work is performed?

6.4
HOW DO LIVING CELLS RELEASE ENERGY FROM FOOD?
Active cells need more energy to do their work than inactive
ones. Check this by comparing germinating pea seeds with
dormant pea seeds. This experiment takes several days. Set it
up now, then look at the experiment set up by another class.

48

Figure 6.3

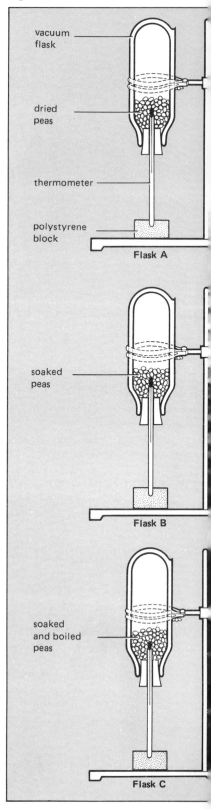

Dry peas
Soaked peas
Soaked and boiled peas

Labels and card
3 vacuum flasks fitted with corks and thermometers (-10 to $110\,°C$)
3 clamp stands and polystyrene blocks

1 Set up the apparatus as shown in figure 6.3. Use dried peas in flask A and peas soaked overnight in flask B. In flask C put peas that have been soaked, boiled for 10 minutes, and then allowed to cool.

2 Label the flasks.

3 Draw a results table on a card and arrange a rota for filling in the temperature during the next three or four days.

4 Examine the results of a similar experiment set up three or four days ago.

Q 12
Which flask showed a rise in temperature?

Q 13
Explain why this is a sign that energy was being transferred.

Q 14
a What change can be seen in the peas where energy had been transferred?
b What kind of work has been done? (See section 6.2.)

Q 15
Why didn't the peas in the other flasks release energy? (Clue: read about enzyme activity on worksheet FSM 8b or in section 12.7.)

The changes which occur when energy is transferred from food are summarized below.

$$\text{Food + oxygen} \xrightarrow{\ -\ \text{energy}\ } \text{carbon dioxide + water}$$

If these changes happen quickly, for example when burning is involved, all the energy comes out as heat (with a little light energy), and the temperature shoots up.

Inside living cells, the energy-storing food molecules are broken down, bit by bit. This involves many chemical changes, each controlled by its own enzyme. The transfer of energy is slow.

Energy in the body is used in three ways: for making materials needed for cell growth; for electrical current to work nerve cells; and for contracting muscle cells. Some heating occurs with every energy change, but much less than when food is burned.

Q 16
Why is heat useful to humans and other warm-blooded animals?

Figure 6.4

6.5
WHICH NUTRIENTS STORE ENERGY?

Carbohydrates (starches and sugars), fats, and proteins are the constituents of our food which store energy. Alcohol is another energy store included in many diets.

Q 17
In what form do these three constituents of food enter the cells in the body:
a carbohydrates
b fats
c proteins?

Most cells can make use of all these sources of energy. Brain and nerve cells are different. They must have glucose for their energy supplies. The glucose supply to the brain and nerve cells must be kept constant. After a meal has been digested, some of the glucose absorbed into the blood is stored in the liver as *glycogen*. Between meals, the liver changes glycogen back to glucose so that the blood glucose level does not fall. If it did, the brain would be without its energy supply — a potentially fatal condition.

Q 18
Glycogen is an insoluble carbohydrate. Why does this make it a better food store than glucose?

Q 19
a What is the food material in most plant food stores?
b Name *three* different plant food-storage organs which are harvested for human food?

Q 20
Animals move about and have to carry their food stores inside their bodies. What would you expect a suitable energy storage material for animals to be like? (Look at table 6.1 for clues.)

Figure 6.6
Carrying food stores:
a *spring lambs*
b *mackerel.*

	Energy available per gram	
	kcal	kJ
Carbohydrates	3.75	16
Fats	9	37
Proteins	4	17
Alcohol	7	29

Table 6.1
Food energy values of nutrient

The fatty tissues in the human body are our longterm energy stores. They form a safeguard against food shortages which were likely to affect our ancestors during some seasons of the year. In the poorest countries of the World, sections of the population suffer serious food shortages, particularly when crops fail.

Figure 6.5
Food stores in plants:
a *bananas*
b *potatoes*
c *ears of wheat.*

Figure 6.8

Q 21
a Why are body fat stores less important in Western countries now than they were two hundred years ago?
b Do you think that some people have no need of any form of longterm energy store?

The body makes its fat stores from fragments of nutrients not needed for immediate energy release. These fragments can come from *any* of four sources: fatty acids, glucose, amino acids, or alcohol.

The fat in your fat stores comes not only from fat in your diet; extra starches, sugars, proteins, and alcohol all provide identical nutrient fragments which the body can build up into fats for storage.

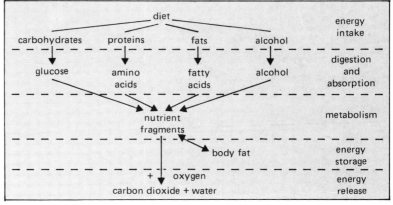

Figure 6.7
How energy-giving nutrients contribute to the pool of nutrient fragments.

Q 22
What would happen to the stores of body fat of a person who became ill and could not eat?

6.6
DO YOU FEEL FULL OF ENERGY?

The transfer of energy, according to the scientists' definition, is what enables work to be done. Feeling 'full of energy' means, in everyday language, feeling ready for an activity of any sort — whether you call it work or play. Eating regular meals which satisfy hunger and build up stores of body fat will supply you with enough energy for all your activities. But that won't make you feel energetic at all times. Indeed, eating a good meal might have the opposite effect of making you feel sleepy! What you have in your body is plenty of *stored energy*. Before it can be any use it has to be transferred from that store.

Releasing energy from nutrients in cells is complicated. Four different kinds of nutrients have to be broken down into fragments. Many chemical changes are involved. Each change will only work if it has its own special enzyme. All these different enzymes have to be made inside the cells. To make these enzymes, three of the B group vitamins are needed: thiamin (vitamin B_1), riboflavin (vitamin B_2), and nicotinic acid (niacin).

If the diet does not supply enough of these enzyme-linked vitamins, cells will have difficulty in transferring energy from food. Thiamin deficiency can be very serious, causing the deficiency disease called *beri-beri*.

Q 23
a Which nutrient depends on a thiamin-linked enzyme for its breakdown?
b Which cells of the body depend on this nutrient for their energy supply?
c Which parts of the body are likely to be affected in the disease beri-beri?

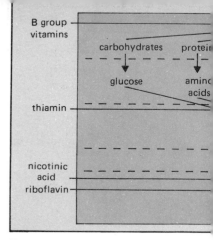

Figure 6.9
How vitamins operate the processes of metabolism and energy release.

'Most of the nutrients needed in the diet will be provided if a wide variety of foods is eaten, including some unrefined foods.' This is a quotation from section 3.1. It explains why most people living in Western countries have no need to worry about thiamin intakes and why poor communities in Eastern countries risk beri-beri on a diet of polished rice and little else.

Q 24
a How is rice polished?
b What happens to its nutrient composition (see table 6.2)?

Q 25
a Why do you think people like polished rice?
b How does the practice of polishing rice compare with how we use our cereal staple in Britain?

Q 26
a What non-nutrient substance is taken into the body and used in energy release?
b What is the disease which prevents enough of this substance being carried in blood?
c What symptom would you expect to occur with this disease?

	Rice, unpolished (per 100 g)	Rice, polished (per 100 g)
Energy (kcal)	345	352
Protein (g)	8.0	7.0
Fibre (g)	0.5	0.2
Calcium (mg)	10.0	5.0
Iron (mg)	2.0	1.0
Thiamin (mg)	0.25	0.06
Riboflavin (mg)	0.05	0.03
Nicotinic acid (mg)	2.0	1.0

Table 6.2
Nutrient composition of rice.

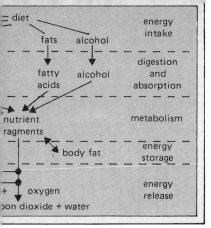

Figure 6.10
Gerry Staunton finishing a mini-marathon.

BACKGROUND READING

A DIET FOR CHAMPIONS

Athletes have always been fussy about their diets. Sparta, the Olympic sprint winner in 668 B.C., is said to have trained on dried figs. Dromeus of Stympholeus who won the long race in 460 B.C. and 456 B.C., and later became a trainer, made his pupils train on meat. Today many weight lifters and throwers swear by high protein foods to build up muscle strength during training. For these athletes steak, eggs, and milk account for a large part of their shopping bills. A number of athletes are also keen on vitamin supplements, especially vitamin E. As events are so competitive, that little bit extra speed or distance can make all the difference between winning and losing. But how much evidence is there that diets can help performance? The short answer is — very little. In general there appears to be no special diets or nutrients that help athletes perform better.

One possible exception is the 'carbohydrate loading diet' for endurance events such as cycling or marathon running. During long events the main fuel used for energy is muscle glycogen. In theory, if an athlete builds up his muscle glycogen store he will have an advantage. One way of doing this is to get rid of all muscle glycogen by exercising vigorously one week before the competititon and for the next three days to eat almost nothing but fat and protein. In the time that's left lots of carbohydrate should be eaten. Experiments show that muscle glycogen can be increased by two or three times like this and maximum work times can go up by as much as 50 per cent. A further advantage of this diet is that because glycogen holds water there is more water in the body. One of the problems with endurance events is dehydration, so this extra water can help. A recent study of 123 marathon runners showed that of the 56 who put themselves on a carbohydrate loading diet before the event, very few were dehydrated or needed a drink at the end of the race.

Gerry Staunton is a competition marathon runner. His best time is 2 hours, 16 minutes, and 37 seconds (the World record is 2 hours, 8 minutes, and 43 seconds). This makes him about the 25th fastest in Britain. In an average year, he runs three or four marathons and perhaps ten to twelve half marathons. On top of this he runs a hundred miles a week in training. Gerry, who comes from Gallway in Ireland, is often asked by race organisers or his national team to run in events all over Europe. Although Gerry isn't too worried about what he eats, he has developed his own sort of carbohydrate loading diet. One or two days before the race, he will eat extra helpings of high-carbohydrate foods. His one complaint about marathon running is that he is always hungry.

Though this approach to diet seems to work for Gerry it should not be adopted by anyone else without consulting a doctor. No diet which is devised for a special purpose is appropriate for everyday circumstances.

53

CHAPTER 7

How much food energy do we need?

Figure 7.1
This woman doing light work is expending energy at an average rate of 425 kJ per hour.

7.1
ENERGY FOR BODY WORK

Your body is using energy at all times throughout your life, but at different rates depending on the work being done. It is useful to think of:

maintenance body work, which goes on automatically and continuously;

performance work, which can be started and stopped at will.

Maintenance body work provides the back-up for performance work. Body processes which go on automatically include:

pumping blood round the body;
breathing air in and out of the lungs;
digesting and absorbing food, breaking it down in cells;
getting rid of unwanted materials in urine;
making new materials for tissues and secretions;
brain and nerve activity;
maintaining correct concentrations of body fluids;
maintaining a constant body temperature.

Q 1
Name *five* body systems which work automatically. Can any of these be made to work faster or slower at will?

Performance work which is only done for some of the time includes:

moving the whole of the body, as in walking;
moving parts of the body, as in chewing;
using sense organs deliberately, as in reading.

Figure 7.2
The energy expenditure rates of these swimmers will be much lower than the rate of 2000 kJ per hour for competition swimmers.

Q 2
Most performance work is mechanical, that is, concerned with movement and lifting loads. Which type of body structure is always involved?

When resting in bed, or fully relaxed in a chair, the body is only doing maintenance body work. The rate at which energy is then being used is called the resting metabolic rate (R.M.R.). This is usually measured in kilojoules per minute. The value of your R.M.R. will depend on many factors, including body size and whether or not you are growing.

Q 3
Which will require more energy, pumping blood around the body of a tall or a short man?

Q 4
How will the large amount of chemical work being done in the body of a growing child affect its R.M.R?

As soon as you sit up, extra muscles start contracting and you use energy at a faster rate — your metabolic rate increases above R.M.R. The amount of extra energy being transferred when performance work is being done will depend on how heavy the loads being moved are and how far you have to carry them. Remember that you use your muscles to carry your body about — probably the heaviest load you are likely to lift!

Q 5
a Why does it take more energy to do a job standing up than sitting down?
b Name two jobs in the home which are often performed standing up which could be done sitting down.

Q 6

If a man and a woman, each of average height and weight for their sex, took a walk together, which would use more energy? Why is this?

When performance work is being done by the body, maintenance body work is also going on, but not at resting rates. Find out what happens to the rate at which the maintenance organs work when performance work is being done by your body.

‖‖ YOU WILL NEED: ‖‖‖

Stop watch   Step-up stool
Clinical thermometer   Comfortable seat

With the class in pairs, one member of each pair should act as the subject and the other as the recorder.

1 Each member of the pair should practise feeling the other's pulse at the wrist, using finger tips not the thumb, and counting the beats. Decide how to detect breathing movements or sounds, and also check on how to use the clinical thermometer.

2 With the subject seated comfortably, thermometer in mouth, the recorder should count the subject's pulse in beats per minute. Also record the body temperature and ask for the subject's own description of temperature sensations.

3 The subject should now take between 2 and 5 minutes' vigorous physical exercise.

4 With the subject once more comfortably seated, the recorder repeats the measurements and observations in instruction 2.

5 Repeat instructions 2, 3, and 4 with the roles reversed. Record your results in a table like the one below.

Figure 7.5

Figure 7.4
Pulse taking: use finger tips, not the thumb.

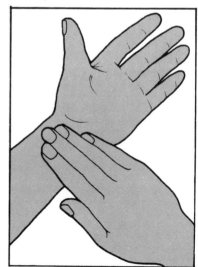

Subject		John Smith	Mary Jones
Pulse beats per minute	before		
	after		
Breaths per minute	before		
	after		
Style of breathing	before		
	after		
Body temperature	before		
	after		
Subject's feelings	before		
	after		
Subject's appearance	before		
	after		

Q 7
What evidence have you obtained to support the statement that increased performance work increases the rate of maintenance body work?

Q 8
What substances were being supplied to muscles in increased amounts during vigorous physical exercise?

When muscles are used for mechanical work, energy from food is needed not only for this work but also to speed up the maintenance body functions of blood circulation, breathing, chemical breakdown of food, and removal of waste.

Total energy needed = energy for performance work + energy for maintenance body work

When athletes are training they are trying to increase the proportion of energy used for performance work. But even in the best trained bodies, only about 25 per cent of the energy transferred is used in doing mechanical work. The rest of the energy (75 per cent or more) speeds up the body's maintenance processes and is changed into heat.

Q 9
a What happened to your body temperature during vigorous exercise?
b What evidence did you obtain that the energy used to speed up body processes is changed to heat?

7.2
ENERGY FOR BODY WARMTH
In Chapter 6 it was stated that energy is never destroyed, only transferred from one thing to another. All energy eventually ends up as heat (extra kinetic (moving) energy of the particles of nearby substances including air). This extra kinetic energy corresponds to a rise in temperature of the substance. When the energy becomes shared out among a very large number of particles, the rise may not be very noticeable.

When energy is transferred from food to make the body work, the heating effect is usually more than enough to keep the body temperature constant. Look again at your results in figure 7.5. It is quite likely that subjects will say that, after vigorous exercise, they felt warm or possibly hot. But what effect had this on the body temperature?

To prevent the body temperature rising when the body is active, an efficient cooling system is needed. Some subjects will have become red in the face through vigorous exercise, some will have started to sweat. Before answering questions 10 and 11, make some simple observations.

Figure 7.3
Using a step-up stool.

Figure 7.6
Losing excess heat after hard physical exercise.

cotton wool
and surgical
spirit

Figure 7.7

Figure 7.8
Keeping baby warm.

Small quantity of surgical spirit
Cotton wool

Thermometer to read atmospheric temperature
Clinical thermometer

1 Measure the temperature in the classroom (the thermometer should not be in direct sunlight) and compare it with the temperature inside the mouth (already taken in section 7.1).

2 Work out the temperature drop between your body and its surroundings.

3 Use the cotton wool to dab surgical spirit on to the back of one hand. Watch what happens to the liquid.

4 Record the sensation in the back of that hand.

Q 10
a Why is heat likely to pass from your skin to the surrounding air?
b How can heat be brought from inside the body to the skin?
c What evidence is there that this happens more with vigorous exercise?

Q 11
a What was taken from the skin to make the surgical spirit evaporate?
b Why is sweating important in keeping the body's temperature from rising above normal?

Q 12
a What is the reflex response by muscles to feeling cold?
b How effective is it?

During waking hours, if you avoid cold rooms and wear suitable clothes, you will get more than enough heat from the energy being used by the body. The process of *thermogenesis* (direct conversion of food energy into heat) is only necessary when we are completely at rest, usually asleep. The bodies of people who are fit and well switch to thermogenesis when necessary. Babies, very old people, and ill or very tired people do not respond sufficiently and can suffer from *hypothermia* (the inability to keep the body temperature up to normal level).

Q 13
Is it necessary to have heated bedrooms for everyone?

Thermogenesis can also occur when you are not feeling cold. This wastes energy — but that is hardly a problem for many people in rich Western communities who frequently overeat!

7.3
MEASURING ENERGY EXPENDITURE
Measuring energy expenditure must take account of all work done and any heat wasted.

Total energy used in a day	=	total maintenance body work	+	total performance work	+	extra heat from thermogenesis

Because energy transfer and work are equivalent, both are measured in the same units.

Measuring all the energy used in a day for the many different kinds of work sounds complicated. Fortunately *all* energy used eventually gets changed into heat — and heat can be trapped and measured.

Q 14
How was the energy expenditure of germinating peas detected? (See section 6.4.)

Q 15
a Why was this only *detection* and not measurement of energy expenditure?
b What else would need to be known for a measurement of energy?

When scientists measure the energy expenditure of a living organism, they construct a chamber, called a *respiration calorimeter*, in which the plant or animal can live normally. All the heat produced is trapped and measured.

The results obtained are very dependable, but respiration calorimeters for humans are very expensive to construct and run, and only indoor physical activities can be tested. An easier method of estimating energy expenditure involves measuring oxygen used (see worksheet NM9).

Q 16
What evidence did you obtain in section 7.1 which indicated that oxygen consumption could be directly related to energy expenditure?

Portable respirometers, for measuring oxygen use, can be worn by people doing their ordinary jobs. The data on energy expenditure rates shown in the table on worksheet NM9 was obtained using both respiration calorimeters and portable respirometers.

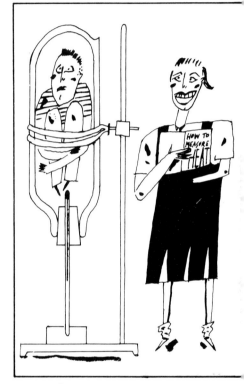

Figure 7.9

7.4
ESTIMATING DAILY ENERGY EXPENDITURE
Nutrition scientists, trying to establish how much food is needed to provide energy for the whole population, have hit upon the idea of defining an 'average' man and woman and an 'average' day.

The 'average' man is 25 years old and weighs 65 kg (10 stone).

The 'average' woman is 25 years old and weighs 55 kg (8½ stone).

The hours and the activities of an 'average' day are set down (or logged) as follows:

8 hours rest in bed;
8 hours in occupational (work) activities;
8 hours in non-occupational activities, covering everyday chores and leisure (both exercise and relaxation).

You can probably think of many people who don't conform to this pattern, and many day-to-day variations in your own life. But on reflection you will realize that the 'average' day provides a framework which can be adjusted to fit most people's lives. Here are examples of energy expenditure by three different people.

Example A
An average man (65 kg) employed in clerical work. He usually goes jogging for one hour and watches television each evening for three hours.

8 hours bed rest and sleep, at 250 kJ/hour	2000 kJ
4 hours everyday chores, at 450 kJ/hour	1800 kJ
8 hours light work, at 500 kJ/hour	4000 kJ
1 hour exercise (jogging), at 1500 kJ/hour	1500 kJ
3 hours relaxation (television), at 350 kJ/hour	1050 kJ
Total	10 350 kJ

This total comes to 10.25 MJ when calculated to the nearest 0.25 MJ.

Example B
An average man (65 kg) employed in non-mechanized farm labouring. His evenings usually include playing darts for two hours and gardening for two hours.

8 hours bed rest and sleep, at 250 kJ/hour	2000 kJ
4 hours everyday chores, at 450 kJ/hour	1800 kJ
8 hours heavy work, at 1000 kJ/hour	8000 kJ
2 hours exercise (gardening), at 900 kJ/hour	1800 kJ
2 hours relaxation (darts), at 450 kJ/hour	900 kJ

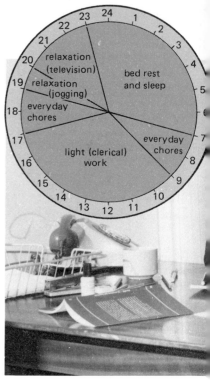

Figure 7.10
Clerical worker.

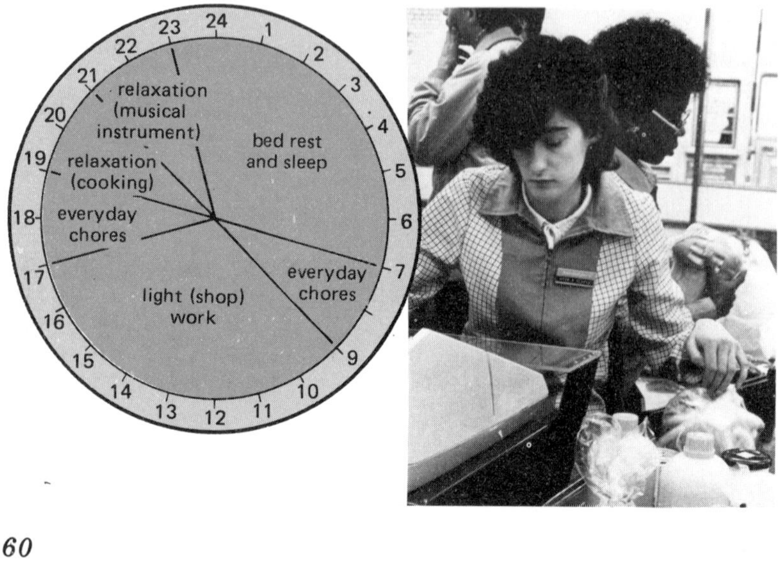

Figure 7.12
Farm worker.

Figure 7.11
Shop assistant.

Q 17
What is the farm worker's estimated energy expenditure in megajoules?

You will have noticed that the main differences in energy expenditure between the two examples are due to their different occupations and leisure activities. It is fairly easy to group people according to occupation, but not according to how they spend their leisure. However, as people grow older they tend to take less strenuous exercise and engage in more restful leisure activities. This is one reason why people's energy requirements decrease with age.

Body weight also affects energy expenditure. On average women weigh less than men. An average woman weighs 55 kg (8½ stone) which is about 15 per cent less than the average man's weight. She will need about 15 per cent less energy for the activities which require her to support her own weight, that is most working activities and all forms of exercise. When calculating energy expenditure for the average woman, rates for occupations and leisure should be reduced by 15 per cent.

Q 18
Why is it only thought necessary to alter energy expenditure rates for periods of occupational activity and exercise?

Example C
An average woman (55 kg) employed in a shop. She usually spends two hours at home in a standing activity (*e.g.* cooking) and two hours in a leisure activity sitting-up (*e.g.* playing a musical instrument).

8 hours bed rest and sleep, at 250 kJ/hour

4 hours everyday chores, at 450 kJ/hour

8 hours light work, at 425 kJ/hour

2 hours relaxation (standing), at 450 kJ/hour

2 hours relaxation (sitting up), at 400 kJ/hour

Q 19
What is the shop assistant's total estimated energy expenditure during an average day? Express your answer:
a   in kilojoules
b   to the nearest 0.25 MJ
c   in kilocalories.

How does your life-style affect your daily energy expenditure?

Decide whether your occupational activities at school are 'light' or 'moderate' and draft an hourly time plan for a typical evenings activities. Then, to make a 24-hour calculation, apply the appropriate values from the energy expenditure tables on worksheet NM9. Remember that you have estimated the energy ex-

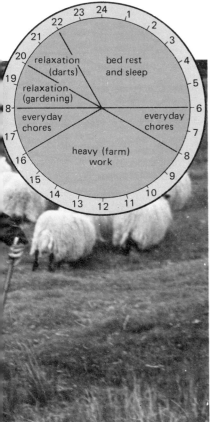

penditure for an *average* man or woman with *your* lifestyle, *not* for you personally. Nevertheless, doing the calculation will tell you a lot about what influences your energy requirements.

7.5
USING R.D.A. OR R.D.I. TABLES
Look at worksheet M18b and pick out the age range and occupational category to which you belong. Now look at the recommendations for energy intake for an *average* member of your group.

Q 20
In what ways do you think you differ from the average for your group?

Q 21
Do you think your energy requirements are average/below average/above average? Give reasons for your answer.

You will also see recommendations for intakes of several of the nutrients.

Q 22
a List the nutrients for which there are United Kingdom recommendations.
b Name some nutrients for which there are no recommendations.
c Why do you think some nutrients are included and not others?

Once food administrators are satisfied that there is enough food to meet the energy needs of a population, they must check on nutrient supplies. The R.D.A. (and R.D.I.) figures are guidelines for amounts of nutrients needed to promote health and prevent disease in very nearly all of the population. Unlike recommendations for energy, R.D.A.s for nutrients are *not* based on average requirements. In fact, the daily amounts recommended are more than most people need.

Figure 7.13
Seebohm Rowntree (1871 - 1954).

BACKGROUND READING

NUTRITION ON THE 'DOLE'
For those unlucky enough to be out of work the trip to the unemployment office to sign on becomes a necessary if unpleasant chore. The money handed out as supplementary benefit has to last until the next cheque arrives. If it's spent too quickly, someone is going to go hungry. How supplementary benefit rates have been worked out makes an interesting story.

In 1899 Seebohm Rowntree set out to discover how many people in York were living in poverty. He surveyed over 11 000 families and asked questions about what each family spent money on. He also took details about housing, health, weight, and height. After speaking to experts, Rowntree decided that a man doing fairly heavy work needed about 3500 kcal per day and that women and children needed a fraction of this. He then worked out a diet which would give this amount of energy for the least cost. The diet took no account of personal taste or palatability and was probably almost uneatable. Along with the minimum cost for housing, rent, and clothing, this diet was used to work out the least amount of money a family needed to live on. Anyone earning less than this was said to be living in poverty.

To be put in this category Rowntree said that, 'A family must never spend a penny on railway fare or omnibus. They must never go into the country unless they walk. They must never purchase a half penny newspaper or spend a penny to buy a ticket for a popular concert. They must write no letters to absent children, for they cannot afford to pay the postage. The children must have no pocket money for dolls, marbles, or sweets. The father must smoke no tobacco and must drink no beer'. Rowntree worked out that 15 per cent of the population of York were living like this.

Figure 7.14
Family living in one room in London, 1901.

In 1935, Rowntree changed his least-cost diet to take some account of people's tastes. The diet was still a long way off what people actually ate. Three years later a politician called William Beveridge started to work out how much the government would have to give people if they were out of work or were not earning enough to live on. He based his calculations on Rowntree's work. As a result of all this the National Assistance Act of 1948 was able to state the amount of supplementary benefit people were entitled to.

Over the years supplementary benefit appears to have kept pace with inflation. However if one looks closer the picture isn't quite so good. Inflation is based on the Retail Price Index. This is the cost of an average 'basket' of consumer goods. The basket contains food as well as luxury items such as washing machines. Because poor families spend a large part of their money on food and the price of food has gone up more than the price of other goods, inflation for poorer families is higher than the Retail Price Index would suggest.

Nowadays, if a family complains that they cannot make ends meet on supplementary benefit they may be told that they are not doing their housekeeping properly.

CHAPTER 8

Food energy: the balancing act

8.1
CAN YOU ESTIMATE YOUR ENERGY INTAKE?

The food tables (worksheet M21) give energy values and nutrient content of standard portions of food. Look at the descriptions of standard portions in the second column and weights in the third column. Some foods have obvious standard portions, such as an egg or a banana, but would you be able to recognize a size 3 or 4 egg or a medium-sized banana? Many standard portions are measured in 15-ml or 5-ml spoonfuls. Do you know what two 15-ml spoonfuls of cabbage or one heaped 5-ml spoonful of jam look like? Practice is needed in measuring out standard portions so that you can readily recognize the *amounts* of food you are eating.

||| YOU WILL NEED: |||||||||||||||||||||||||||||||||||||||||||||||||||||||||||||||||||||

Enough different foods to produce one person's meals for a day, chosen from the foods included in the food tables (worksheet M21).

Food preparation facilities — equipment, utensils, balances, and measures (including 15-ml (table) and 5-ml (tea) spoons)
Materials for displaying prepared food in standard portions — cling-film, labels, felt pens
Calculators
Worksheet M21

Instructions to the whole class
1 With the foods provided, agree on a pattern of meals and snacks for one day and a simple menu which will suit most members of the class.

2 Divide into groups, one group for each meal.

3 Make a results table like the one in figure 8.2 below. Fill in columns 1, 2, and 3.

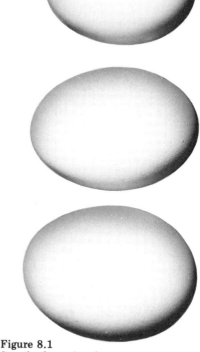

Figure 8.1
Standard portions?
a   *Three eggs.*
b   *Three bananas.*

①	②	③	④	⑤		⑥
Meals pattern	Menu	Standard portion	Number of portions	Energy value		Vitamin A
				kJ	k cal	µg
Breakfast	cornflakes	4 15-ml spoonfuls	1	390	90	O
	sugar	1 heaped 5-ml spoonful	1	170	40	O
	milk	from allowance	–	–	–	–
	coffee + milk	from allowance	–	–	–	–
Mid-morning	potato crisps	1 small packet				

Figure 8.2

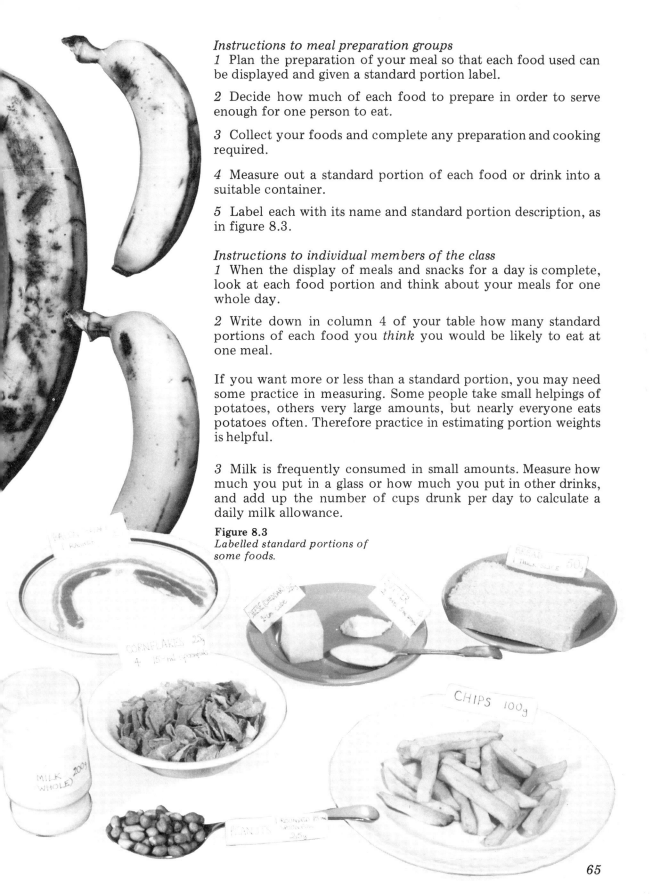

Instructions to meal preparation groups

1 Plan the preparation of your meal so that each food used can be displayed and given a standard portion label.

2 Decide how much of each food to prepare in order to serve enough for one person to eat.

3 Collect your foods and complete any preparation and cooking required.

4 Measure out a standard portion of each food or drink into a suitable container.

5 Label each with its name and standard portion description, as in figure 8.3.

Instructions to individual members of the class

1 When the display of meals and snacks for a day is complete, look at each food portion and think about your meals for one whole day.

2 Write down in column 4 of your table how many standard portions of each food you *think* you would be likely to eat at one meal.

If you want more or less than a standard portion, you may need some practice in measuring. Some people take small helpings of potatoes, others very large amounts, but nearly everyone eats potatoes often. Therefore practice in estimating portion weights is helpful.

3 Milk is frequently consumed in small amounts. Measure how much you put in a glass or how much you put in other drinks, and add up the number of cups drunk per day to calculate a daily milk allowance.

Figure 8.3
Labelled standard portions of some foods.

4 Enter energy values in both kJ and kcal in column 5.

5 Find the total energy value of food and drink *you* expect to consume in a day.

6 Combine with the rest of the class and find the average expected energy intake for one day.

Keep your completed table. You will need it for Chapter 13.

Q 1
a Is your own result above, below, or about the average for the class?
b Suggest reasons why this is so.

Calculating the energy value of what you *think* you will eat gives some evidence of energy intakes. For more dependable evidence, it is necessary to know what you have actually eaten.

Q 2
Have you completed a foods-eaten diary? If so, for how many days? Were they all weekdays or were week-ends included?

Keeping a foods-eaten diary means writing down the amounts of everything you eat and drink. To do this accurately, you have to weigh the food you take and anything left uneaten. Weights must be written down at once. This is a tedious business and sometimes it is inconvenient.

Q 3
In what circumstances would you decide just to write down numbers of standard portions of food and drinks consumed? (You would of course have to be able to recognize standard portions.)

Q 4
Can you think of *two* drawbacks to the 'standard portion' method?

8.2
ENERGY INTAKE AND YOUR R.D.I.
How does your energy intake compare with the recommended daily intake for your age group? When you have calculated your energy intake for two or more days as a homework exercise, you will be able to compare your daily average with the recommended daily intake (R.D.I.) for your age group (worksheet M18).

Q 5
If you found that your intake was below or above the recommendation would you:
1 question the accuracy of your calculations
2 remember that the recommendation is the average for your age group
— and not for you personally
3 wonder whether you ought to adjust your diet?

In fact, the answer is 'yes' to all three suggestions in question 5.

Figure 8.4
His and her ideas of breakfast!

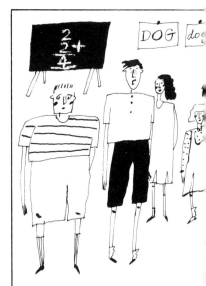

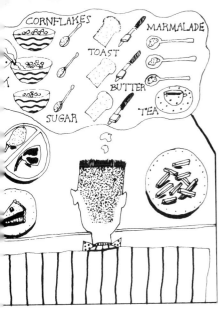

Figure 8.5

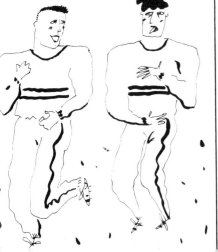

Q 6
How might inaccuracies occur when completing your foods-eaten diary?

Q 7
If you were extremely careful not to eat or drink anything you had not weighed and recorded carefully, you could still end up with an inaccurate calculation for your *normal* daily energy intake. Why?

Examine the illustrations in figure 8.5. Each shows people from the same group in the R.D.I. tables (worksheet M18).

Q 8
a For each of the illustrations, identify the R.D.I. group(s) to which the people portrayed belong. Give your reasons.
b What is the main difference shown in each illustration affecting energy requirements?
c How does each difference have an effect?

Q 9
What is meant by saying that athletic training can increase energy efficiency? (See section 7.1).

Even among untrained people there are variations in energy efficiency. Some people wish their bodies would use energy more wastefully. Their problem is that they don't take a lot of exercise and can afford to buy plenty of food. They have difficulty in balancing intake and output and tend to become fat. They need to consider what action to take.

8.3
HOW MUCH ENERGY DO YOU REALLY NEED EACH DAY?
The amount of energy you need is the amount of energy you use. When the average amount of energy in the food you eat in a day equals the average amount of energy you use in a day for all kinds of work and growth (if any), you have balanced intake and output. Look at figure 8.6.

Figure 8.6

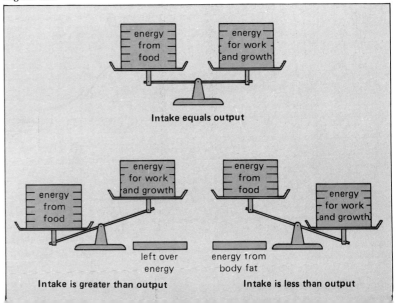

Q 10

List all the kinds of work contributing to energy output. (See section 6.1 and sections 7.1 and 7.2.)

Q 11

How can you tell whether some of your energy is needed for growth? (Look at figure 8.6.)

The energy balance is lost when intake is more than output. The 'left-over' energy is usually stored in body fat. Some people can get rid of excess energy as heat, by the process of *thermogenesis*.

Q 12

How can someone who has stopped growing find out whether they are adding to their stores of body fat?

Q 13

Why must young people look for other signs that fat-stores are increasing?

Q 14

Give *two* ways of getting back into energy balance. (Look at figure 8.6.)

Q 15

a When energy output exceeds energy intake, the difference is made up from body fat. How could someone check that body fat stores are being used up?

b How could they avoid getting misleading results from the measurements taken?

Q 16

Why is it unnecessary to balance intake and output *every* day?

8.4
WHAT IS OBESITY?

In Western societies, it is no longer necessary to store much body fat. The fashionable figure is either athletic or slim. Two centuries ago, being thin was a sign of ill-health or poverty. This is still true in many developing countries. Apart from appearance, there are good reasons for guarding against becoming too fat (or *obese*).

Obesity is defined as: weighing 20 per cent more than the desirable weight for your height and build.

Look at worksheet NM10 which shows tables of 'desirable' weights produced by a life insurance company. The dangers of obesity to health are summarized in table 8.1.

Figure 8.7
The fashionable figure.
a *Early sixteenth century.*
b *Today.*

Type	Effects	Cause
Mechanical	Flat feet, osteo-arthritis in knees, hip, and spine	Heavy loads strain skeletal structure
Metabolic	Diabetes mellitus in middle age, high plasma cholesterol, gall stones	Over loaded fat stores
Cardio-vascular (heart and blood)	High blood pressure, tendency to heart disease	Extra effort required for blood circulation
Respiratory	Bronchitis, sleepiness	Breathing difficulties, CO_2 retention
Accidental	Falls	Ungainly movement
Psychological	Unhappiness	Poor self-image

Table 8.1
Possible dangers to health from obesity.

Q 17
Why are life insurance companies interested in producing desirable weight-for-height tables?

	Percentage obese
Men over 30	20
Women between 30 and 60	20
Women over 60	30
Infants	15
Pre-adolescent children	5
Adolescent boys	10
Adolescent girls	20

Table 8.2
Obesity in the United Kingdom.

Obesity is common in al! wealthy countries. Many doctors believe that obesity is more common in Britain now than 40 years ago.

Q 18
a Why can't they be sure?
b What would they need to know in order to prove their opinion?

Mechanization has reduced the amount of energy required by most people during the past 40 years. Evidence of energy intakes is available from government statistics (figure 8.9).

Q 19
a Are people consuming more, less than, or about the same amount of energy as they were 40 years ago?
b Do you think that this will balance people's energy needs today?

Many older people are obese now because they have been overeating over the past twenty years or so.

Q 20
Is there any indication from figure 8.9 that there might be less obesity in Britain in the future? Suggest a reason why this might be so.

8.5
SENSIBLE SLIMMING
All health experts are agreed that the problem of obesity should be tackled by dietary control of energy intake. Increasing energy output by taking more exercise will help (and should be encouraged), but it is not enough to change fat people into slim people. Most people have to cut down on exercise as they become older. But if good eating habits are developed early on, they can continue throughout life. Planning a good weight-reducing diet means selecting foods for each day which:
1 supply less energy than is being used so that some body fat is used up
2 supply enough of all the essential nutrients
3 satisfy appetite and are pleasant to eat
4 are easy to prepare at home or select from a canteen.

Q 21
a Which are the energy-supplying components of foods and drinks?
b Which of these have high energy values? (See section 6.5.)

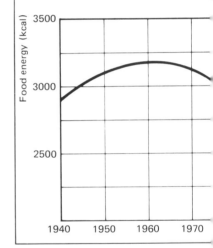

Figure 8.9
Average food energy consumption per person per day in the United Kingdom.

Figure 8.11

Figure 8.8
Mechanization.
a *Getting to school today.*
b *Getting to school 40 years ago.*
c *Laundering today.*
d *Laundering 40 years ago.*
e *Ploughing today.*
f *Ploughing 40 years ago.*

Figure 8.10
Slimming aids.

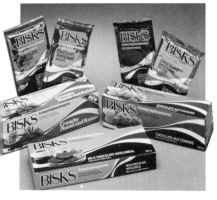

This is the reason for restricting the amounts of fatty foods and alcoholic drinks in the diet, and for learning which are the high-fat foods. (See section 3.3).

Q 22
Which foods supply one of the energy-giving nutrients and nothing else?

Energy-only foods can be cut down in the diet without risking a shortage of essential nutrients.

Q 23
Why can unrefined foods play an important part in an energy-restricted diet?

Q 24
What particular advantage is there in the consumption of unrefined foods from plants?

Commercially produced slimming aids usually contain substantial amounts of added cellulose. Sugar is replaced with chemical sweetners such as saccharine.

A slow, steady weight reduction from a diet which is easy to stick to is more successful in the long run than a 'crash' diet. This might have dramatic results after a few days, but will be difficult to keep up.

When you are trying to keep to a diet which will reduce your weight, it is important to remember not only which foods to choose but also the amounts to be eaten.

Q 25
Why is familiarity with standard food portions a good help to slimmers?

People starting a slimming programme need encouragement from family and friends. Some people find weight reduction difficult because they use food energy economically. Any surplus of intake over output is stored as body fat and not turned to heat by thermogenesis. These people might feel envious of others who eat more and yet never seem to put on weight. Nutritional scientists are researching into why people are so different in this respect. They have some evidence which indicates that people who easily put on weight have less than other people of a tissue, called brown fat, which is involved in thermogenesis.

Slimming, however, can sometimes bring harmful results. A serious disorder called *anorexia nervosa* occurs when weight reduction is carried too far. Those affected are unable to appreciate when a desirable weight has been achieved and go on rejecting food. Their bodies suffer as in starvation and, if treatment is not accepted, death will follow. Most (80 per cent) of those diagnosed are girls in their teens, many of high intelligence. Fortunately, this disorder is widely recognized and help is available for sufferers.

8.6
CHOOSING BETWEEN ENERGY SOURCES
If you get your energy balance right, and all the nutrients are present as well, does it matter where the energy comes from?

Figure 8.12 shows the approximate proportions currently obtained in Britain from the energy-giving nutrients.

Government statistics on food supplies collected during and since the Second World War allow us to study changes in food consumption.

Examine the graph in figure 8.13, and look for patterns in consumption of the three main sources of food energy.

Q 26
What do you notice about the percentage of energy from protein?

Q 27
What happened to the percentage of energy from fat every time the percentage of energy from carbohydrates changed?

Q 28
How did the energy pattern change between 1940 and 1970?

Doctors concerned about heart disease, which is a greater problem now than in the 1940s, think that the shift towards fat and away from carbohydrates ought to be reversed. They support the dietary guideline to reduce fat intakes and recommend that fats should contribute not more than 30 per cent of our energy. Not all fats are alike. Saturated fats are the ones linked with heart disease and as far as possible they should be replaced by polyunsaturated fats (see Chapter 15 and *Food Science*, Chapter 8).

Carbohydrates are not all alike either. Sugar, from sugar cane or

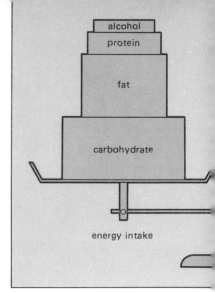

Figure 8.12

Figure 8.13
Sources of energy in the United Kingdom diet.

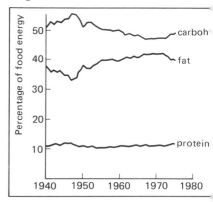

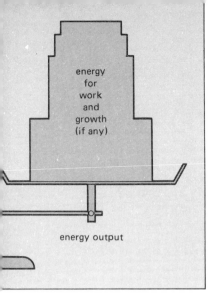

energy for work and growth (if any)

energy output

Figure 8.14
Sugar substitute.

Figure 8.15
Fitness classes are part of the slimming business.

sugar beet (with the chemical name *sucrose*), is closely linked with dental caries. Hence the dietary guideline to reduce intakes of sugary foods. This can be followed *either* by learning to prefer less sweetening in foods *or* by using sugar substitutes. Recipe adaptation is necessary because sugar produces texture changes in cooked foods. In your next food preparation session, you could practise both approaches.

Figure 8.13 omits any data about energy from alcohol. Only in the last decade has its consumption been sufficiently widespread for it to count as an energy source in the *average* diet. Anyone who is trying to cut down on energy intake should remember the high energy value of alcohol.

Q 29
What is the energy value of the alcohol in:
a a glass of beer
b a glass of dry wine?

Everyone who drinks alcohol at all should remember that alcohol dependence is as great a danger to health as over-consumption of any of the nutrients already mentioned.

BACKGROUND READING

THE SLIMMING BUSINESS
Slimming is a big business. At any one time something like 35 per cent of British women are trying to lose weight. In 1978 £80 million worth of slimming-aid foods were sold in Britain alone — 70 per cent of these were sold to women. Women in particular are made to worry about their weight. Every time they turn on the television or open a magazine there is sure to be a very thin actress or model staring out at them.

Because there is no easy way to lose weight, would-be slimmers are always on the look out for some miracle cure in the form of a tablet or injection — anything that's easier than will-power. Doctors are often asked to prescribe *appetite suppressant diuretics* (these make you lose water but not fat). Saunas and Turkish baths have become common meeting grounds for the weight-conscious, but once again the effect is only water loss. There can be very few slimmers who have never dreamed of the wonder drug that burns away all unwanted energy (always referred to in the publicity as 'calories'). Unfortunately, scientists have yet to make the break-through.

There are many slimming products available in shops. They include starch blockers which are supposed to stop digestion of starch by blocking the action of digestive enzymes. This probably only works in a test-tube. High-protein, low-calorie powders replace whole meals and are claimed to make you lose fat, but doctors are by no means convinced of this. Another aid is the 'appetite suppressant'. Some of these contain fibre which expands when taken with a liquid. In theory this should make you full up, but the general view is that the tablets

73

don't contain enough fibre to do the job properly. In a survey, only 13 per cent of those who tried appetite suppressants found that they helped. Other suppressants aim to raise blood-sugar levels and so affect a part of the brain which controls appetite. Many people who have tried say the effect does not last very long.

There are some products available which may be some use. Meal substitutes, like the chocolate bar or pack of biscuits with added vitamins and minerals, can help as they tell you exactly how much energy is eaten. The trouble is that eating chocolate and biscuits is not a good way to learn sensible eating habits. Calorie-counted prepared meals, available in packets or tins, may be more useful as it can often be difficult to calculate the energy supplied when you prepare a cooked meal yourself. The most useful items are probably the low-energy food substitutes like 'Sweetex' sugar, 'Marvel' milk, and 'Outline' margarine, as they can be used both during and after a diet. Funnily enough, you can quite easily end up paying more for the privilege of consuming less energy!

CHAPTER 9

Where there's life there's protein

9.1
FOODS AND NUTRIENTS

Although this chapter is all about proteins, it must be remembered that when we eat a food we usually eat a mixture of nutrients. White sugar is an exception. It's pure carbohydrate!

Meat is often called a 'protein' food, but it contains water, fat, vitamins, and minerals as well as protein. Cereals are often called 'starchy' foods. This is very misleading as they contain protein, fat, vitamins, and minerals as well as starch.

9.2
PROTEINS AND LIVING THINGS

Proteins are an essential part of all living organisms. Life on earth would not exist without them.

Figure 9.1
Nutrient mixtures:
beans on toast
and a glass of milk.

Figure 9.2

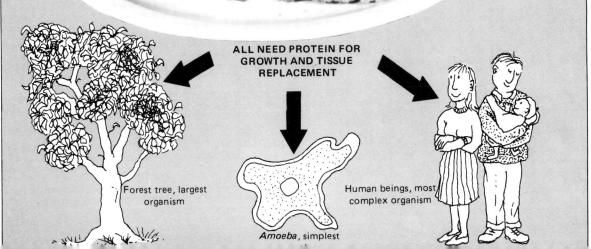

ALL NEED PROTEIN FOR
GROWTH AND TISSUE
REPLACEMENT

Forest tree, largest
organism

Amoeba, simplest

Human beings, most
complex organism

Q 1
What is the name of the substance which contains protein inside all living cells? (*Clue:* see section 2.4.)

Proteins are present in every part of our bodies. Proteins with compact molecules can be moved around in the water of body fluids, and proteins with long thread-like molecules twist together to make fibrous structures like hair and connective tissue. Muscle proteins can get shorter and make muscles contract; skin proteins can be stretched like elastic; enzyme proteins can make chemical reactions happen inside the body; chromo-proteins can carry oxygen around the body; and there are many more:

different proteins — in different places — for different purposes.

9.3
PROTEIN AND TISSUE STRUCTURES
Each of the many tissues in the body needs the right kind of proteins for its structure. You will be shown some tissues from an animal with similar (not identical) tissues to your own. Watch how the tissues are separated. Bones can be taken out of the meat neatly and safely if a sharp knife is used skilfully.

Now try to separate and label the tissues yourself.

||| YOU WILL NEED: |||||||||||||||||||||||||||||||||||||||||||||||||||||||||||||||||||||||||||||||||||||||||||||||||
Small piece of breast of lamb   Chopping board
                                             Pins and labels with names of tissues
Boning knife   Beaker of dilute hydrochloric acid

1 Copy and complete the table in figure 9.3.

Name of tissue	Description
Muscle	
Fat	
Bone	
Red bone marrow	
Connective tissue	
Cartilage	
Tissue fluid	

Figure 9.3

The description could include the colour, and adjectives such as hard or soft, wet or greasy, fibrous, waxy, rubbery, and watery.

2 Put some breast of lamb bones in dilute hydrochloric acid. The others will be burned in the laboratory. The results will be considered in Chapter 10.

Q 2
Which tissues do you call 'lean' when talking about meat?

Q 3
a Which tissue is made of fine stretchable fibres?
b Why is it found in all parts of the body?

Q 4
All tissues contain other substances as well as protein.
a Which tissue contains a lot of water?
b Which contains a lot of fat?

Q 5
Some body tissues were not present in the tissues you examined. What would you get from the butcher if you wanted to examine some glandular tissue?

Q 6
How is bone different from other tissues?

Later you will be looking at the results of the bone experiment. They will help you to see how proteins function in bone structure.

9.4
PROTEINS FROM PROTEINS

Where do the many different proteins in our bodies come from? If you answered 'from our food', you were nearly right. You should have said 'from the proteins in our food'.

But, the proteins in our food are not exactly the same as the proteins in our bodies. Food proteins have to be broken down into amino acids which are later put together in the right arrangements for body proteins.

Q 7
Where, when, and how are food proteins broken down?

Q 8
a Where are amino acids built up into body proteins?
b How do they get there?

There are twenty different kinds of amino acids in food proteins which are used in body proteins. Only eight kinds of amino acids *must* come from the diet and these are called *essential amino acids*. The others can be made in the body.

The best quality food proteins contain the eight essential amino acids in the amounts needed for body proteins to be made without wasting amino acids.

Lower quality food proteins contain all the eight essential amino acids but in amounts different from the body's needs. When these proteins are used, extra amounts are needed to keep cells supplied with those essential amino acids which are in short supply. Other essential amino acids are left over and are switched to energy supplies.

Cells stop making protein if one essential amino acid runs out. The essential amino acid likely to run short first is called the *limiting amino acid*. Each lower quality food protein has a limiting amino acid.

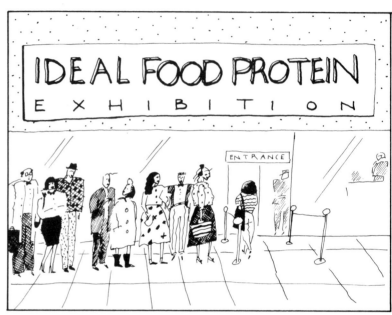

Figure 9.4

9.5
WHAT IS AN IDEAL FOOD PROTEIN LIKE?
An ideal food protein would have all the amino acids present in just the amounts needed for making body proteins. There would be no limiting amino acid. It could be used without any amino acids being wasted. Therefore less of an ideal protein would be needed than other proteins. Knowing what an ideal food protein is like is useful because other food proteins can be compared with it and the limiting amino acids detected. A lot of experiments have been done to find the pattern showing relative amounts of essential amino acids. Scientists working for the United Nations Food and Agriculture Organization think the ideal food protein would have essential amino acids in amounts shown in figure 9.5.

The columns in the histogram show the relative amounts of eight kinds of amino acid which the body needs to have at the same time to make its proteins. Other amino acids are used as well, but the body can make them if necessary.

High quality proteins will have as much or more of each of the eight. Lower quality proteins will have a limiting amino acid — the one present in the smallest amount compared with the ideal.

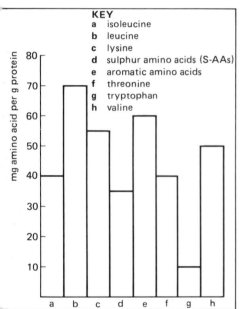

KEY
a isoleucine
b leucine
c lysine
d sulphur amino acids (S-AAs)
e aromatic amino acids
f threonine
g tryptophan
h valine

Figure 9.5
Amino acids in an 'ideal' protein.

9.6
FINDING THE LIMITING AMINO ACID

||| YOU WILL NEED: ||||||||||||||||||||||||||||||||||||||||||||||||||||||||||||||||||||||||||||||||||||||
Tracing paper or transparent film   Worksheet NM11
                                      Ruler
Fine coloured pencil or felt pen

1 Look at the histograms on worksheet NM11. Check that each food protein contains some of each amino acid. Amino acids have names (look at the key), but you won't have to remember them all!

2 Trace the outline of the pattern of amino acids in an 'ideal' protein (figure 9.5) in a bright colour.

3 Place your tracing over each histogram in turn. For each food protein, compare amounts of amino acids with 'ideal' amounts. If some are less than ideal, try to spot the limiting amino acid (the one which will run short first).

4 Draw a table like figure 9.6 and fill in your results.

	Amino acids in ideal amounts or more	Amino acids in less than ideal amounts	Limiting amino acid
Whole wheat	b, d, e, g	a, c, f, h	c–lysine
Rice	a, b, d, e, g, h		
Maize			

Figure 9.6

Figure 9.7

Q 9
a Which food proteins have no limiting amino acid?
b What group name fits all these foods?

Q 10
a Which food proteins have limiting amino acids?
b In which group do these foods belong?

Q 11
Which is the limiting amino acid for cereals?

Q 12
a What does the abbreviation S-AAs stand for?
b What food proteins are limited by S-AAs?
c What is the group name for these foods?

9.7
CHOOSING FOODS FOR AMINO ACID SUPPLIES
The results you found after working through section 9.6 will probably make you think that the best way of getting all the amino acids you need in the right amounts is to eat animal foods.

Figure 9.8
Cereal foods and pulses are important sources of protein.
a *Pasta.*
b *Mung bean salad.*

Certainly the proteins in meat, fish, eggs, and milk are high quality and many of us like eating them. But there isn't enough animal food in the World for everyone to get enough. In any case plants do provide protein, and some people prefer plant to animal foods. Cereals and pulses (peas, beans, and lentils) are the most important sources of plant proteins because they contain quite large amounts compared with fruits and other vegetables. (Check this statement in your food tables, worksheet M21.) Also, the production of plant proteins can be more efficient than the production of animal proteins and makes better use of the land available (see table 2.1).

Q 13
a Which of the foods in table 2.1 can be produced on a commercial scale in the United Kingdom?
b Which of these makes best use of agricultural land in terms of protein production?

The problem with cereal proteins is their shortage of lysine. If you had to get all the lysine your body requires from cereals alone you would have to eat very large amounts. Other amino acids would be wasted. We want to avoid wasting amino acids if we possibly can because foods which contain them are generally expensive.

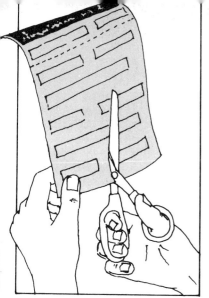

Figure 9.10

Figure 9.9
Many people enjoy getting protein from animal foods.
a *Bacon and eggs.*
b *Milk.*

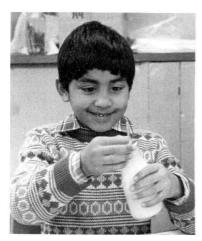

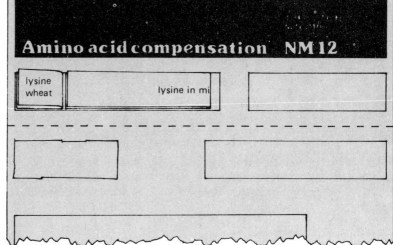

Figure 9.11

In pulses it is the sulphur amino acids (S-AAs) which are in short supply. Even if you had enough of one plant food to get all the lysine or S-AAs needed, eating one food only would be boring. Interesting meals include a variety of foods. Find out what mixing does to amino acid patterns.

||| YOU WILL NEED: ||||||||||||||||||||||||||||||||||||||||||||||||||||||||||||||||||||||||||||||||||||||||||
Worksheet NM12
Pair of scissors
Ruler

1 Look at the bars on worksheet NM12. Their lengths show amounts of lysine or S-AAs in patterns for the 'ideal' protein, wheat protein, beans protein, and milk protein.

2 Cut out the six bars below the dotted line.

3 Place the cut-outs over the bars for 'ideal' protein to check that wheat protein has less lysine and beans protein has less S-AAs than the 'ideal'. The other proteins all have more.

4 Look at the amounts of limiting amino acids in mixtures of wheat and other food proteins. Wheat is an important staple; maximum value should be made of its proteins by mixing it with a good source of lysine. Try a half-and-half mixture of wheat and milk proteins. Fold bars for wheat lysine and milk lysine in half. Lay them end-on over the 'ideal' lysine bar as shown in figure 9.11.

Check that the wheat and milk mixture gives nearly as much lysine as 'ideal' protein. Do the same for sulphur amino acids using S-AAs bars for wheat and milk folded in half and placed on the S-AAs bar for 'ideal' protein. Record results in a table like figure 9.14. Use phrases like 'more', 'about equal', 'a bit less', and 'much more'.

You will have discovered that wheat and milk give a good protein mixture. But, for some people in the World, milk and other animal foods are scarce. Other people may wish to avoid any food which comes from an animal.

5 Some plant foods eaten together give good amino acid mixtures. Try a half-and-half mixture of wheat and beans protein.

Repeat instruction 4, but use the bars for beans protein instead of milk protein. Record results and try to decide whether wheat and beans proteins are better eaten together or alone.

Do you ever eat wheat and beans together? What about beans on toast? In the proportions usually served, the mixture is about one-third wheat and two-thirds beans proteins.

6 Try this out with your folded paper strips. Use a ruler to divide the strips into thirds before folding. Record results and decide whether this mixture is as good as or better than half and half.

Good protein mixtures can be made from plant foods with different limiting amino acids. Even better mixtures occur when animal protein is added. Only small amounts are needed so that the cost is not greatly increased.

7 Try this with a mixture of one-third wheat protein, one-third beans protein, and one-third milk protein. Record results.

Figure 9.12

Protein mixture	Lysine compared with ideal	S-AAs compared with ideal
$\frac{1}{2}$ wheat / $\frac{1}{2}$ milk		
$\frac{1}{2}$ wheat / $\frac{1}{2}$ beans		
$\frac{2}{3}$ beans / $\frac{1}{3}$ wheat		
$\frac{1}{3}$ wheat / $\frac{1}{3}$ beans $\frac{1}{3}$ milk		

Figure 9.14

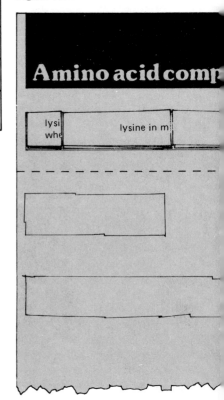

Q 14
a Why do wheat and milk give a good protein mixture?
b Name *two* popular food mixtures based on wheat and milk proteins.

Q 15
Why is it better to eat a mixture of wheat and beans than either food alone?

Q 16
Does the proportion of wheat protein to beans protein make any difference?

Q 17
a Why is the one-third wheat protein, one-third beans protein, and one-third milk protein the best mixture tested?
b Calculate the protein in one-and-a-half thick slices of wholemeal bread, in three heaped 15-ml (table)spoons of baked beans, and in one glass of milk.
c Why do these figures suggest a high quality protein mixture?

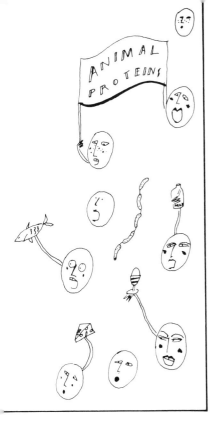

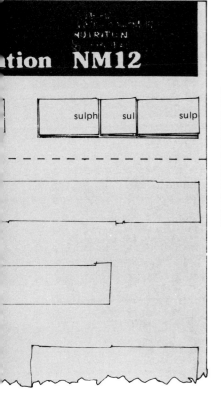

Figure 9.13

Q 18
Give two reasons why animal sources of protein are highly valued.

Q 19
Why is it possible to be healthy without eating any animal foods, provided there are sufficient plant foods available?

9.8
PLANNING FOR GOOD PROTEIN VALUE

Wheat, beans, and milk were chosen as examples of foods to work with because wheat is a cereal, and all cereal proteins are limited by lysine; beans are pulses, all of which have proteins which are limited by S-AAs; and milk is one of the animal foods with no limiting amino acids in their proteins.

But it is not necessary to eat only three foods! When planning high value protein meals, the lessons learned in section 9.7 can be applied with any mixtures of cereal and animal proteins; cereal and pulse proteins; and cereal, pulse, and animal proteins.

Q 20
How could you vary the 'beans on toast plus glass of milk' idea for a snack? Make *three* suggestions for snacks or dishes which each contain cereals, pulses, and animal foods.

Cereals have been included in each of the mixtures considered so far. This is because, for many people, cereals are the main staple crops. But some countries use other crops, such as potatoes. We need to know about both the *quantity* and the *quality* of the protein in the staple of someone's diet before advising on food choice. Table 9.1 shows the quantity of protein as grams per 100-gram servings of some cooked staples.

	Protein, g per 100 g
Boiled potatoes	1.4
Boiled yams	1.6
Stewed plantain	0.5
Boiled spaghetti	4.2
Cassava porridge	1.0
Boiled rice	2.2

Table 9.1

Q 21
a Which are cereal and which non-cereal foods in table 9.1?
b How do the two groups compare for protein quantity?

When a community has to depend on a staple with a low quantity of protein there is a risk of protein deficiency. This is greater when food is scarce. When someone does not eat enough food to meet their requirements for energy, any protein in the diet goes to supply energy and not for making body protein.

(Look at Chapter 6 for a reminder about energy being released from amino acids.) Protein-energy malnutrition is a serious problem among children in the World's poorest countries.

BACKGROUND READING

THE WORK OF THE HEALTH VISITOR

Health visitors are qualified nurses who have undergone a further year's study specializing in the prevention and early detection of disease. Most of their work concerns children, particularly the under fives. They are also involved in ante-natal care, the school health programme, health education in schools and community groups, and the health care of the elderly. Health visitors work closely with doctors and, through them, become involved with patients with such problems as diabetes, high blood-pressure, and obesity. The health visitor is in an excellent position to reach a broad section of the population to give advice on health matters.

Teaching about healthy eating begins well before a baby is born. The unborn baby is entirely dependant on the nourishment supplied by the mother's bloodstream. It is very important that the mother is careful about what she eats or drinks during pregnancy so that she and her baby are as fit as possible. The health visitor will advise her about the dangers of smoking, drinking alcohol, and taking unprescribed medicines, and encourage her to eat wisely, so that she does not put on too much weight. She will also encourage her to breast feed her baby to give it the best start in life.

At about 4 months old, most babies start on solid foods. The health visitor will advise on the most suitable food and emphasize the importance of not adding salt or sugar. Young children are often fond of sweets and biscuits. These are very bad for their teeth. They can often be persuaded to have a piece of fruit or raw vegetable instead. Once at school, the problem of discouraging bad eating habits becomes greater as children are influenced by their friends and the local tuck shop. The health visitor, either directly or through the teacher, then has to impress upon them the reasons why a good diet is important, even though the problems of adulthood seem very far away. This attitude is the key to the greatest problem in preventative medicine: to make people realise that the way they live now will determine their health and happiness in the future.

Figure 9.15
A health visitor talking to a group of pregnant women.

CHAPTER 10

Calcium and vitamin D

10.1
WHAT KIND OF MATERIAL IS NEEDED FOR BONES?

If you had to choose the material for making your bones, you would begin by deciding on the properties which would be right for the jobs that bones have to do.

Q 1

From the many different shapes and sizes of bones, you would expect them to do different jobs. What is the most obvious purpose of
a the long leg bones
b the bones of the skull?

Bones also provide secure attachments for muscles and for the surfaces (covered by cartilages) which move against each other in joints. Long bones can be used as levers for lifting things.

Q 2

What *two* properties would you expect in a material which has to perform all these functions?

Q 3

Look back to section 9.3. How did you describe bone tissue?

Q 4

What kinds of damage must bone material be able to resist?

The experiments on bones should help you to understand why bone material is ideal for its purpose.

‖‖ YOU WILL NEED: ‖‖‖
Breast of lamb bones: untreated, ashed, and demineralized

2 mounted needles
Hand lens

1 Examine the bone samples and compare them with the bones in figure 10.2.

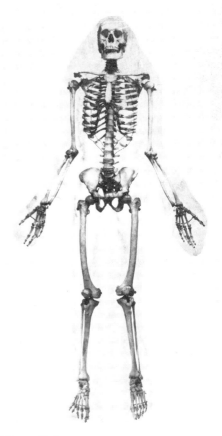

Figure 10.1
Human skeleton.

Figure 10.2
a *Untreated bones.*
b *Demineralized bones.*
c *Ashed bones.*

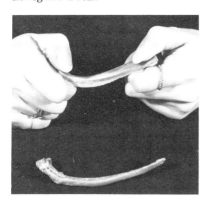  

2 Use the needles to tease out the demineralized bone and the hand lens to look at the structure of bone ash.

Q 5
a Describe the texture of ashed bones.
b Describe their strength.

Q 6
a How would you describe the texture of demineralized bones?
b Describe their strength

Q 7
What evidence is there that untreated bone combines the properties of ashed bone with the properties of demineralized bone?

Closer examination of the demineralized bone will show that it is made of fibres. These are formed from the protein *collagen*, which also forms the fibres of connective tissue (see section 9.3).

Fibres in animal tissues are chemically different from fibres in plant tissues. This can be shown by burning some animal fibre and some plant fibre and testing the gases given off.

IIII **YOU WILL NEED:** IIIIIIIIIIIIIIIIIIIIIIIIIIIIIIIIIIIIIIIIIIIIIIIIIIIIIIIIIIIIIIIIIIIIIIIIIIIIIII

Small samples of untreated bone	Tongs
Hair or wool	Red and blue litmus papers
Cotton or paper	Bunsen burner
	Goggles
Ignition-tube for each material being tested	Flameproof mat

1 Place a very small sample of each material in an ignition-tube.

2 Strongly heat each sample in a Bunsen burner flame, holding the ignition-tube horizontally with tongs. Wear goggles. ⚠

3 When fumes start to come out of the ignition-tube, hold first a red and then a blue strip of moist litmus paper at the tube mouth.

4 Record any colour change. Say whether each material was acid or alkaline. (Alkaline fumes turn red litmus blue; acid fumes turn blue litmus red.)

5 Try to detect the smells by wafting fumes gently and carefully towards your nose. Smells are best described by comparison with familiar materials when burning.

Fibrous material	Origin (animal or plant)	Acid or alkaline fumes	Smell
Untreated bone	animal		
Hair	animal		
Cotton	plant		

Figure 10.5

Figure 10.6
Calcium compounds:
a *carbonate in chalk rocks*
b *sulphate in blackboard chalk*
c *phosphate in bone ash.*

Figure 10.3

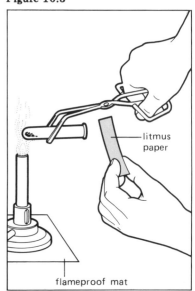

litmus paper

flameproof mat

Figure 10.4

Q 8
How can fibres from animal tissue be distinguished from plant tissue fibres?

Q 9
Why do fibres from animal foods not behave like dietary fibre in the digestive system?

The acid-resistant remains of bone were referred to as *de-mineralized*. This means that the acid treatment has removed the mineral matter. Your description of the ashed bones (question 5a) might have included the word 'chalky' and chalk is a mineral. Whether you mean the sticks used for writing on a blackboard or the rock which forms the cliffs of Dover, chalk is a compound of the mineral element calcium — so is the ash from bones.

Bones are not the only parts of the body which contain calcium. Teeth are formed in a similar way to bones, but they have more calcium phosphate and less protein. This is why teeth are harder than bones. Calcium is also found in the blood. It has an important part to play in blood clotting. In muscle tissue fluid, calcium is necessary for the stimulation of muscle contraction.

10.2
WATER SOLUBILITY OF CALCIUM COMPOUNDS

Q 10
Would you expect a water-soluble or water-insoluble form of calcium in
a bones
b teeth
c blood
d tissue fluid?

Many calcium compounds are insoluble in water, but they can be changed into soluble forms.

Q 11
What was the effect of dilute hydrochloric acid on bone (see section 9.3)?

Q 12
How could you show in an experiment that bone ash is insoluble in water but soluble in dilute hydrochloric acid? Include details which would help your demonstration to be quick and clear.

Q 13
a Where in the digestive system are insoluble calcium compounds in food made soluble?
b Why is this necessary?

Calcium dissolved in water is in the form of ions, which are very small particles, each with a double positive charge. If there are negative ions around, they will be attracted by calcium ions and could link up to form insoluble calcium compounds. Try this with some solutions of calcium compounds.

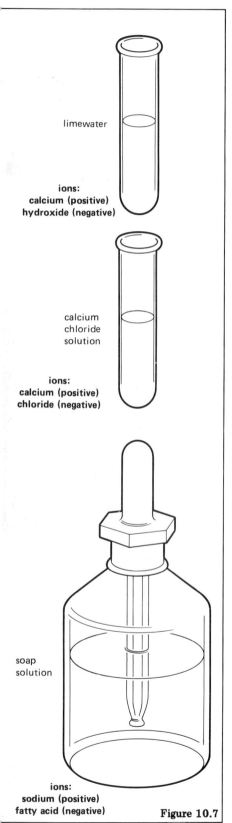

limewater

ions:
calcium (positive)
hydroxide (negative)

calcium
chloride
solution

ions:
calcium (positive)
chloride (negative)

soap
solution

ions:
sodium (positive)
fatty acid (negative)

Figure 10.7

IIII YOU WILL NEED: IIIIIIIIIIIIIIIIIIIIIIIIIIIIIIIIIIIIIIIIIIIIIIIIIIIIIIIIIIIIIIIIIIIIIIIIIIIIIIIIIIIIIIII

½ test-tube of lime water (solution of calcium hydroxide)
½ test-tube of calcium chloride solution
Soap solution in a dropping bottle

Test-tube rack

1 Add soap solution, drop by drop, to both test-tubes. Rock the test-tubes gently to mix the contents.

2 Continue until a change is clearly seen.

Q 14
What evidence is there of the formation of insoluble material?

Q 15
Why would you expect the insoluble substance in both test-tubes to be formed from calcium ions and fatty acid ions?

Q 16
a Where in the digestive tract are fatty acid ions formed?
b Why are they likely to prevent some of the calcium in food being absorbed?

Only part of the calcium in the diet is ever absorbed. Other negative ions in the small intestine, such as phytate and oxalate, link with calcium to form insoluble compounds which pass out of the body in the faeces. Fortunately, enough calcium will get through to the blood stream if good sources of calcium are included in the diet and if the body has enough vitamin D.

10.3
CALCIUM IN THE DIET
You can get some idea of your average daily needs for calcium from worksheet M18b.

Q 17
Why is it stated clearly that these are recommendations for population *groups* in the United Kingdom?

Q 18
Why are recommendations for daily amounts of calcium greater for children and babies than for adults?

Recommendations for nutrients such as calcium are based on the average requirement for each group plus an allowance to cover the needs of nearly all members of the group. This means that the recommendations will be more than most members of the group require. These excess amounts are unlikely to be harmful, whereas inadequate intakes would be.

Use worksheet M21 to find the important sources of calcium in your diet.

IIII YOU WILL NEED: IIIIIIIIIIIIIIIIIIIIIIIIIIIIIIIIIIIIIIIIIIIIIIIIIIIIIIIIIIIIIIIIIIIIIIIIIIIIIIIIIII
Worksheet M21
Pen and paper

1 Decide how many milligrams of calcium per standard portion counts as a rich source.

2 List all the foods which have at least this amount.

3 Go through the list and cross out any foods which you rarely or never eat.

4 Look again at the food tables (worksheet M21). Are there any foods with a low calcium content which you eat often enough for them to be an important source? Add these to your list.

5 If rhubarb or spinach are on your list, cross them off. They contain oxalate.

Q 19
Why don't foods containing oxalate count as good sources of calcium?

Now that you have completed your list, try to classify the foods so that they can be remembered easily. Invent your own headings or use those in figure 10.8.

Milk and foods made with or from milk	White bread and foods made with white flour	Fish with bones

Figure 10.8

Q 20
a Which important sources of calcium would you reject if you were a vegan?
b What could be used in their place?

The information in the food tables assumes that all white flour (other than self-raising) contains added calcium carbonate. Adding to a food in this way (called *fortification*) was started during the Second World War when milk and cheese were in short supply. It has continued long after these and other calcium-rich foods became readily available again. Without a legal requirement for fortification, it would not be possible to depend on white bread for most of your calcium supply.

Figure 10.9
School milk increased calcium supplies for children when milk and cheese were rationed.

Table 10.1

	Calcium, mg per 100 g
White flour (plain)	15
Fortified white flour (plain)	140
Bread made with fortified white flour	100

Q 21
Using the data in table 10.1, estimate the amount of calcium in bread made with non-fortified white flour. Give your answer in mg calcium per 100 g bread.

Q 22

Which would contain more calcium: a thick slice (50 g) of bread from a loaf made from non-fortified white flour or a thick slice (50 g) of wholemeal bread?

Wholemeal flour has never been fortified with calcium or any other nutrients. It has many advantages over white flour — but one disadvantage. Wholemeal flour contains more phytate than white flour.

Q 23

Why is this a disadvantage?

When used to make bread, much of the phytate in wholemeal flour is destroyed by a yeast enzyme — so the disadvantage is not serious.

10.4
VITAMIN D IN THE DIET

Calcium ions, with their double positive charges, can be attracted and held by the negative charges on some proteins. This calcium binding can happen in the food mixture as it is digested in the small intestine. The trapped calcium ions cannot form insoluble calcium compounds.

Active absorption of calcium from the small intestines uses a special calcium-binding protein which can carry calcium through into the blood stream. Vitamin D is needed to stimulate production of the calcium-binding protein by the cells which line the small intestine.

Vitamin D is present in only a few fatty foods (see table 10.2).

	Vitamin D, μg per 100 g
Natural foods	
Herring (raw)	22.5
Mackerel (raw)	17.5
Salmon (Pacific, canned)	12.5
Sardines (canned)	7.5
Tuna (canned)	5.8
Egg (whole)	1.75
Butter	0.76
Cheese (Cheddar)	0.26
Milk (summer)	0.03
Milk (winter)	0.01
Fortified foods	
Margarine (domestic)	8.0
Fish liver oils (medicinal)	
Halibut liver oil	more than 500
Cod liver oil	more than 125

Table 10.2
Vitamin D content of some foods.

Figure 10.11
Exposing skin to sunlight.

Figure 10.10
Sources of vitamin D.

Figure 10.12
Rickets (the child in the middle is normal).

Q 24

Suggest *two* generic names for classifying the dietary sources of vitamin D which would help you to remember them.

Q 25

Which of the foods listed in table 10.2 occur regularly in your diet?

10.5
VITAMIN D IN THE BODY

Looking at worksheet M18b, you might think that only young mothers should be concerned about vitamin D in their diet and in their children's diet. For an explanation, read footnote *f* below the table.

Q 26

Which groups might have no need of dietary sources of vitamin D?

Q 27

Which groups are likely to need a daily intake of 10 μg vitamin D
a during winter months only
b throughout the year?

The key to getting plenty of vitamin D in our bodies is the exposure of skin to sunlight. Ultraviolet radiation from the sun penetrates the skin and converts a substance in the fat under the skin into vitamin D.

Vitamin D circulating in the blood is changed first by the liver and then by the kidneys into a hormone (a 'chemical messenger') which stimulates the lining of the small intestine to make calcium-binding protein.

10.6
PROBLEMS AND SOLUTIONS

Too little vitamin D in the bloodstream of babies and growing children means that not enough calcium will be absorbed from food for proper bone formation. In severe cases of vitamin D deficiency, the bones are not rigid enough to support the increasing body weight and become mishapen. Knock-knees or bow legs are the result.

In children, this vitamin D deficiency disease is called *rickets*.

Rickets used to be very common in Britain until, in the early 1920s, the cause and cure were discovered. By 1960, better diets, nutritional supplements, and changes in dress and leisure had provided the solution to the problem.

Q 28

a What nutrients would you expect to be supplied in a 'better diet' for bone formation?
b Name *one* food which would supply all these nutrients.
c Why were nutritional supplements also necessary?

Q 29

a Why was cod-liver oil chosen as the nutritional supplement supplied free for babies and young children at the time of food rationing?

b Suggest a reason why pregnant and nursing mothers were given tablets instead.

Q 30

What changes in dress and leisure pursuits contributed to the decline in rickets between 1900 and 1960?

During the 1960s, just when it seemed that the rickets problem had been fully solved, cases of rickets began to be reported again. Most were among the children of Asian immigrants who had settled in northern industrial cities, such as Bradford and Glasgow.

The adult form of rickets (*osteomalacia*) was also reported among Asian women of child-bearing age. Many immigrants are vegetarians. Some do not use margarine or the available welfare foods (vitamin drops for children up to five years old and vitamin tablets for mothers before and after the birth of a baby). The British climate and the traditional dress of Asians could also increase the risk of vitamin D deficiency.

Q 31

a Why is the family in figure 10.14 at greater risk from rickets or osteomalacia than a family which has always lived in Britain?

b Why should they be encouraged to take advantage of the nutritional supplements available under the welfare foods scheme?

Fortunately both rickets and osteomalacia can now be detected before bones become deformed. Doctors and health visitors can recognize the symptoms (usually bone pain and weakness of leg muscles). Treatment of young children using vitamin D supplements is very successful, even for those with bone deformities.

Like all body tissues, bone is constantly being renewed. After the age of 40, the very hard and dense bone is gradually replaced by a more porous form. This is a normal change which causes no discomfort. In some older people, usually women, bones become fragile and fracture easily. The condition, known as *osteoporosis*, cannot be prevented but can be slowed down if levels of calcium in the blood are kept up.

Q 32

Why does medical advice to older people include drinking milk and keeping up outdoor activities?

BACKGROUND READING

HOME ECONOMICS IN THE SOCIAL SERVICES

Kate Norbury is the county home economist for Warwickshire social services department. The department deals with a wide variety of people, including the young, the very old, the

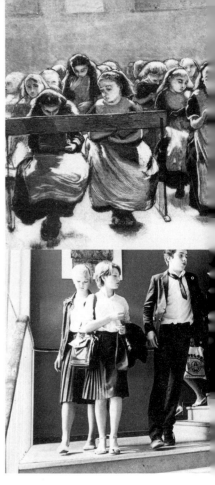

Figure 10.14
Asian family dressed for winter in Britain.

Figure 10.13
School uniform.
a *Victorian.*
b *Today.*

Figure 10.15
The fun of food.

mentally and physically handicapped, and those in care. Kate's work helps to provide a good diet for all the people in the department's care.

The social services have to provide food in a wide variety of circumstances. These include individual prepared frozen meals for lunch clubs or 'meals on wheels', and large-scale catering in residential homes. The nutrient content of menus is checked, and Kate may have to think of improvements which are acceptable and practicable. For example, could evaporated milk be used in milk puddings for extra vitamin D? Could faggots be produced to improve the iron content of meals? Is the dehydrated potato used fortified with vitamin C?

Where fresh food is being prepared in large residential homes Kate discusses good cooking methods with the staff. They consider how to minimize the time between the preparation and serving of food, and how to avoid too many sweet, fried, and salty foods. At each home Kate checks that the food provided meets the R.D.I.s for the groups catered for.

In smaller homes, Kate likes to encourage people living there to participate. Children and handicapped people help with choosing, preparing, and cooking healthy diets for themselves. Young mothers in her care are helped and encouraged to put into practice advice from health visitors and clinics about feeding their babies.

Kate regularly talks to home helps as they often have to prepare and cook food in people's homes. They need to know what is good value on the supermarket shelves and, for example, how much better it is to encourage the elderly to have a high fibre breakfast than to spend money in the chemist's on laxatives.

Food choice is particularly difficult for an elderly person bewildered by the multitude of different foodstuffs available today. Kate's answer to this is to discuss the foods they ate fifty or sixty years ago. Most of them can still be bought. They are less exciting but may be more nutritious than the newer processed varieties.

Nourishing food is only a part of what is involved in eating. For food to be enjoyed, it should look good, taste good, and not be too expensive or take many hours to prepare. Kate plays a part in getting this message across. Leaflets on choosing food for health and good recipes are produced to be given to those in the department's care. With encouragement from social workers, home helps, and voluntary workers, people can be helped to help themselves.

Kate believes that the dietary health of the individual is a large part of the overall quality of life. She is sure that her work on the diets of those at risk in society can make a contribution to their happiness.

CHAPTER 11

Iron and some B vitamins

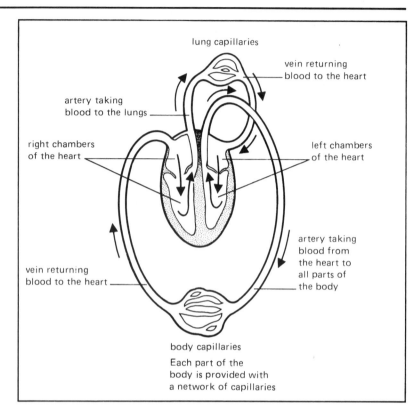

Figure 11.1
Plan of the blood circulation system in a mammal.

11.1
IRON IN THE BLOOD

The heart pumps blood through the arteries and into capillary networks in every part of the body. Veins bring it back to the heart to be recirculated. A blood supply is essential for the working of every part of the body. There have been many references to the functions of blood in previous chapters.

Q 1
What part does blood play in the supply of nutrients to active cells?

Q 2
What part does blood play in getting waste materials out of the body?

These functions depend on the ability of water in blood to disperse particles of nutrients and waste. Another very important function depends on the structure and composition of blood. This function was not studied when breast of lamb tissues were examined in Chapter 9. This is because no blood is left in meat — it is drained out of carcasses following slaughter. But you can easily spare a drop of your own blood for examination with a microscope.

MICROSCOPIC EXAMINATION OF BLOOD

IIII YOU WILL NEED: IIIIIIIIIIIIIIIIIIIIIIIIIIIIIIIIIIIIIIIIIIIIIIIIIIIIIIIIIIIIIIIIIIIIIIIIIIIIIIIIIIIIIIIIIIIIIII

Cotton wool soaked in antiseptic
(*e.g.* Dettol)

Sterilized sewing needle
Microscope

Microscope slide and coverslip
(clean and dry)
Mounted needle
Worksheet M27

1 Squeeze the little finger of your left hand (right hand, if you
are left-handed) between finger and thumb. Prick the tip of the
finger with a sterilized sewing needle. Notice the colour and
consistency of your blood. (If you can't get a drop of your own
blood, someone else in the class will probably supply a drop of
theirs!)

2 Put one drop of blood at one end of the microscope slide.

3 Lower a coverslip over the drop of blood using a mounted
needle (see worksheet M27). Push the coverslip gently towards
the centre of the slide so that a thin film of blood is spread
between the slide and the coverslip (see figure 11.2).

4 Dab your pricked finger with the antiseptic cotton wool.

5 Examine the slide under the microscope; first under low
power magnification, then under high power (see worksheet
M27). Compare what you see with figure 11.3.

Figure 11.3 is a photograph of a slide of blood which has been
stained to show up the white cells. Notice their darkened nuclei.
The white cells on your slide will not be visible without added
stain. The shape of red blood cells is shown in figure 11.4.

Q 3
How would you describe blood seen with the naked eye?

Q 4
How would you describe blood after looking at it through a microscope?

Blood is a liquid which contains masses of tiny cells, most of
which are shaped like a disc. The liquid part of blood is called
plasma. The disc-shaped cells are called *red blood cells* and these
contain the red iron compound *haemoglobin*. Oxygen in the
lungs gets attached to haemoglobin and is carried to all parts of
the body as the red blood cells move through arteries, veins, and
capillaries.

There is iron in plasma as well, though you cannot see any evidence of it. Plasma carries a soluble form of iron to parts of the
body which need it.

11.2
IRON IN OTHER TISSUES
Blood is not the only tissue in the body which contains iron. All
cells need small amounts of iron to provide the chemicals which
control their energy supplies. In addition, muscles have a special

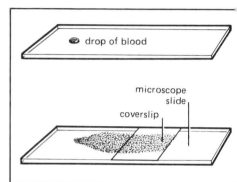

Figure 11.2

Figure 11.3
Photomicrograph of blood cells.

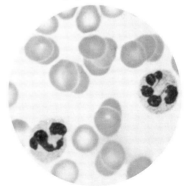

Figure 11.4
Red blood cell (× 9000).

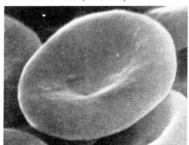

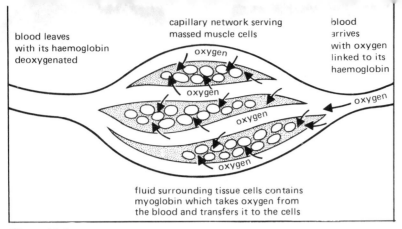

Figure 11.5
Oxygen flow to muscles.

iron compound called *myoglobin*. This is similar to haemoglobin. It is red in colour and can also pick up oxygen. Muscles need large amounts of oxygen. Their myoglobin is used to attract oxygen from haemoglobin in red blood cells across capillary walls and transfer it to muscle cells (see figure 11.5).

Q 5
What gives meat its colour?

Myoglobin is not contained in special cells but is dissolved in the tissue fluid surrounding muscle fibres.

Q 6
What would you do to prove that the red 'drip' from thawing meat is tissue fluid and not blood?

Some tissues store iron. The liver stores an iron compound called *ferritin*. The red bone marrow in the spongy inside of bones contains stores of haemoglobin as it is the tissue in which red blood cells are made.

11.3
WHAT HAPPENS TO IRON IN THE BODY?
You may be surprised to learn that only a small amount of the iron in the food we eat is used by the body. Most of it is passed

Figure 11.6

Figure 11.7
Butcher's shop window including a food made from blood.

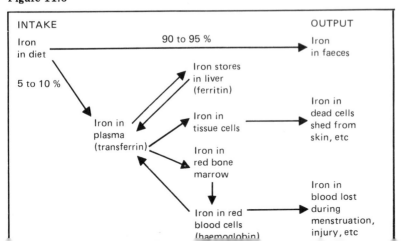

INTAKE		OUTPUT
Iron in diet	90 to 95 % →	Iron in faeces
5 to 10 %	Iron stores in liver (ferritin)	Iron in dead cells shed from skin, etc
	Iron in plasma (transferrin)	Iron in tissue cells
	Iron in red bone marrow	
	Iron in red blood cells (haemoglobin)	Iron in blood lost during menstruation, injury, etc

out in the faeces. Only a small amount is absorbed into the blood plasma. The percentage of iron absorbed varies with different people and can be as low as 5 per cent.

Q 7
If a person has an average daily intake of 12 mg iron and an absorption rate of 10 per cent, what weight of iron is likely to enter the blood plasma per day?

Iron in blood plasma is taken either to cells which need it for their own chemical processes, or to red bone marrow to make haemoglobin for new red blood cells. Any extra iron is stored as ferritin. Red blood cells are constantly being made because they only live about 120 days. When they are broken down, the iron from their haemoglobin is returned to the plasma and then to the liver to be stored as ferritin. In this way the body conserves its iron. Losses due to cells being shed from the skin and internal surfaces are very small. Only when bleeding occurs can losses of iron be considerable. Regular losses of iron result from menstruation in girls and women.

11.4
IRON IN THE DIET
The iron in your body and in the bodies of other mammals is very similar.

Q 8
Which edible parts of the bodies of cattle, sheep, and pigs would you expect to be good sources of iron in the diet?

Q 9
a What happens to the blood from a carcass after slaughter?
b What food can be made from blood? (See figure 11.7.)

Foods from the carcasses of mammals are not the only sources of iron in human food. An egg contains the iron needed by the chick. Plant cells have their own kinds of iron compounds. When selecting foods we need to know how they compare as sources of iron.

Q 10
What facts do you need to know about foods before you can compare them as sources of any particular nutrient?

COMPARING SOURCES OF IRON IN YOUR DIET

YOU WILL NEED:
Worksheets NM14 and M21

1 Look at the list of foods on worksheet NM14 and the description of portion sizes. If you think your usual portion would be larger or smaller, adjust the amount in column 2 before filling in iron contents in column 3 using worksheet M21.

Figure 11.8
All the iron (and other nutrients) needed for this chick's development were provided in the egg.

2 Think how frequently you would eat these portions of food and select your own 'frequency of eating' factor for each food using the table below. Enter the factors in column 4.

Frequency of eating	Factor
Every day	4
Once a week	3
Once or twice a month	2
Occasionally	1
Never	0

Table 11.1

3 For each food, multiply the figure in column 3 by the figure in column 4. Put the answers into column 5. These results are a useful way of comparing foods as sources of iron in the diet.

4 Fill in column 6 with one of the four words which describe the foods as sources of iron in *your* diet. Use the following ratings.

Foods with scores of 3.5 and over are 'important' sources.
Foods with scores of 1.0 to 3.4 are 'useful' sources.
Foods with scores of less than 1.0 are 'poor' sources.
Foods with scores of 0.0 are 'useless' as sources of iron.

Q 11
How could you change a 'useful' source of iron in *your* diet into an 'important' source?

11.5
ABSORPTION OF IRON
It might seem wasteful for so small a proportion of the iron in food to be absorbed into blood plasma (figure 11.6). In fact, this is a safeguard. Too much iron in the body would be harmful. Fortunately, the body can adjust its iron absorption rate according to its needs. When the body's iron stores are low, the absorption rate increases; when they are full, the absorption falls again.

The iron in some foods is more easily absorbed than in others. Iron in the form of haemoglobin and myoglobin is called *heam iron*. This is the easiest to absorb.

Q 12
Which of the foods listed on worksheet NM14 contain haem iron?

The amounts of non-haem iron which are absorbed can depend on other substances in food eaten at the same time. Phytates in whole grain cereals, phosphates in egg yolk, and oxalates in spinach all hinder the absorption of iron. They combine with soluble iron ions in the small intestine making insoluble iron compounds which cannot be absorbed. Extra calcium in the diet can prevent this by 'mopping up' phytates, phosphates, and oxalates before they react with iron.

Vitamin C and proteins in meat help iron absorption. They are reducing agents which turn iron into the form which can be absorbed easily.

Look at your results in column 6 on worksheet NM14.

Q 13
a How well is the iron in your 'important' and 'useful' sources absorbed?
b In column 7, write 'well absorbed' or 'not well absorbed' by each food and say why.

Q 14
a How could other foods be used with sources of non-haem iron to improve absorption?
b Make *two* menu suggestions of food combinations which allow iron to be absorbed efficiently.

Q 15
How do you rate spinach as a dietary source of iron?

11.6
HOW MUCH IRON DO WE NEED?
Look again at figure 11.6. The intake of iron in the diet must be enough to replace the output. It must also be enough to provide for the extra tissue cells and the extra blood needed by babies and children because they are growing. During pregnancy and lactation, enough iron must be available for the growth of the baby and the production of milk.

Look at worksheet M18b. This shows D.H.S.S. recommended daily amounts of nutrients for groups of people in the United Kingdom.

Q 16
Why is the amount of iron recommended for nine- to seventeen-year-olds greater than that for adult men?

Q 17
Why is more iron recommended for women aged between 18 and 54 than for men of the same age and for women over 54?

Worksheet M18b shows recommended *daily* amounts, but, for iron intake, there is no need to worry if some days you eat more and some days less — provided the *average* daily amount is enough. If you eat a rich source of iron, the store in your liver will be built up and could last for several days or perhaps even a week. A good plan is to include one or two rich sources of iron in your diet every week.

Q 18
From your calculations on worksheet NM14, which are the foods which are the 'important' or 'useful' sources of iron which you eat nearly every day?

Q 19
Make a list of foods from which to choose your weekly rich sources of iron.

11,7
WHAT CAN GO WRONG?
When too little iron is taken into the body for a long period of time, the result can be *iron-deficiency anaemia*. This is an illness which makes people feel tired all the time. Shortage of iron prevents sufficient haemoglobin being formed.

Q 20
What process in the body is affected by a shortage of haemoglobin?

Anaemic patients may look pale and feel depressed, although they may not complain of any special discomfort. Often they don't know when the illness starts so that it gradually becomes worse. When a doctor diagnoses iron-deficiency anaemia it is often too late to try a change of diet. Iron pills have to be taken, or sometimes iron is injected. Even these methods can take a long time to get haemoglobin levels back to normal.

Iron-deficiency anaemia affects mainly adolescent girls, women who have had several babies in a short space of time, and middle-aged women. These groups all need extra iron to make up for blood losses. Not many men become anaemic, although it can happen to elderly men if they stop eating the foods which have been their main sources of iron.

Q 21
a What symptoms described by a patient will make the doctor think she is anaemic?
b Why might the doctor look inside the patient's eyelid?

Q 22
What blood test result would confirm anaemia?

Q 23
What would be in pills prescribed for an anaemic patient?

Q 24
Why would a dietitian want a chance to talk to mothers *before* their babies are born?

If you are female, you are 'at risk' from iron deficiency at some time in your life. You should be careful to include a rich source of iron in your diet about once a week.

If you are male, you would be wise to know the important sources so that you go on including them in your diet even when you no longer have a hearty appetite.

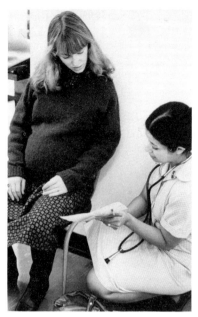
Figure 11.9
A pregnant woman being given advice on diet.

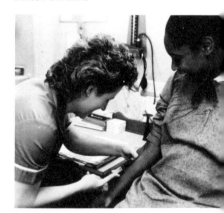
Figure 11.10
Taking a blood sample.

Figure 11.11
Getting pills from the dispensary.

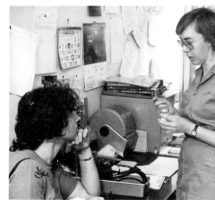

THE DIETITIAN — TALKING TO PEOPLE ABOUT FOOD

Issy Cole-Hamilton works as a dietitian for a community health services department in south London. Here is her description of her job and what she enjoys about it.

'I'll give it a go for a couple of years and then go off travelling again'. That's what I said to myself nearly nine years ago when I started training as a dietitian. Now, all those years, a training course, and two dietetic jobs later, I still love every moment of it.

What is so fascinating about talking to people about food you might ask. Just try it. Food is one of the central points of people's lives. Life depends on it, social situations revolve around it, incomes are spent on it, morale is boosted by it, time is spent preparing and eating it, and religious beliefs are underlined by it.

Most dietitians spend four years training — three years at college and one in hospitals, catering, or the food industry. Once qualified, most dietitians work in the National Health Service. They are employed in hospitals as part of a team. When people are ill, diet is often part of their treatment. For example, people with kidney problems, heart disease, high blood pressure, and diabetes all need special diets to help them stay as well as possible. The dietitian's job is to work with the patient and doctors to design a diet which the patient enjoys and the doctors feel is suitable. The patient is then helped to understand how important the diet is, how to stick to it, and how to make it as easy as possible to continue it at home. After they have left hospital, people often come back to see the dietitian to discuss any problems.

After some time as a general dietitian in a hospital many of us specialize. Some work specifically with children, others with people with kidney problems, the elderly, the mentally ill, or people who are so ill they can't eat at all. Other dietitians do dietetic and nutritional research work.

When I specialized I became a community dietitian. The community dietitian does not work with people who are ill in hospital. My job is to prevent people becoming ill by encouraging them to eat a healthy, well-balanced diet. If you've ever tried to change your eating habits or even 'go on a diet' to lose weight, you will know how difficult it is. My work involves local groups of people, schools, the local authority, other health workers, factories, television, radio, and newspapers. All this includes giving talks, making posters and displays, writing leaflets, and answering questions. A further part of the job is to put research about food and health into the sort of language which everyone can understand.

Even after nine years something new and interesting turns up almost every day, and I'm still wondering when I'm going to get round to going off travelling again.

Figure 11.12
Dietitians Penny Fisher and Issy Cole-Hamilton with part of a nutrition exhibition they designed for hospitals, libraries, and offices.

Figure 11.13
The exhibition ready for viewing.

CHAPTER 12

Potatoes, sailors, and vitamin C

12.1
WHAT IS SO SPECIAL ABOUT VITAMIN C?

When Robin Knox-Johnston returned from his single-handed round-the-world voyage of over ten months, he wrote 'I had vitamin C tablets . . . which I took regularly. I think that the general good health I maintained throughout the voyage could be due to them'.

The potatoes he had taken on board started to go bad after two months. Stocking up with vitamin C tablets proved a wise precaution. But why all this concern for vitamin C — with no mention of the other vitamins? What do you think could have happened to Knox-Johnston if his vitamin C intake had fallen?

Q 1
What function of vitamin C was discussed in Chapter 11?

In cases of prolonged vitamin C deficiency, patients became fatigued and depressed, symptoms which are similar to those of patients with iron-deficiency anaemia.

Q 2
Could there be a link between the symptoms of vitamin C deficiency and iron-deficiency anaemia?

Vitamin C is also needed in the body for the formation of the protein *collagen*. Connective tissue, which is present in all parts of the body, linking cell to cell and tissue to tissue, contains collagen fibres.

Q 3
Chapters 9 and 10 provided opportunities for examination of tissues containing collagen fibres. Which tissues were they and what were their functions? (See section 9.3 and section 10.1.)

Q 4
What do you think would happen if there was insufficient connective tissue?

The disease which results from continued deficiency of vitamin C is *scurvy*. Its clinical signs include swollen and bleeding gums, loose teeth, bleeding below the surface of the skin, delayed healing of wounds, and breaking down of old wounds. These are exactly the effects which could be expected in tissues without enough connective tissue to hold them together. Successful treatment with vitamin C is conclusive proof that scurvy is caused by a diet deficient in vitamin C (see the Background reading).

Figure 12.1
Robin Knox-Johnston with supplies for his ten-month voyage.

Figure 12.3
Taste a few crystals.

12.2
WHAT IS VITAMIN C LIKE?

Vitamin C or, to use its chemical name, ascorbic acid, can be examined and tested to find out what it is like and how it reacts with other things — its physical and chemical properties. Knowledge of these will help you to understand how vitamin C behaves in the body and what is likely to happen to it when foods are cooked or stored.

▥ YOU WILL NEED: ▥▥▥▥▥▥▥▥▥▥▥▥▥▥▥▥▥▥▥▥▥▥▥▥▥▥▥▥▥▥▥▥

Labelled samples of ascorbic acid, citric acid, salt, granulated sugar
Disposable plastic spoon for tasting
Water
Cooking oil
pH test papers
Dilute iodine solution in bottle with dropper
DCPIP test papers

5 test-tubes, with corks, in a rack
Spoon-shaped spatula (or a salt spoon
5-ml (tea)spoon or 5-ml syringe
Glass rod

Figure 12.4

add one spatulaful at a time

shake the test-tube until the crystals dissolve

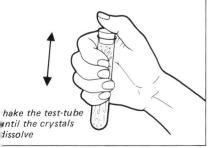

Test	Ascorbic acid	Citric acid	Salt	Sugar	Comments
Appearance					
Taste					
Solubility in 5 ml water					
Solubility in 5 ml oil		—	—	—	
pH of water solution					
DCPIP					
Iodine					

Figure 12.2

1 Draw up a results table like the one in figure 12.2.

2 Describe the appearance of each of the four materials, mentioning colour and physical form.

3 Taste each material in turn. Put a *very few* crystals on the tip of the tongue using the tasting spoon.

Caution: never taste chemicals unless instructed to do so.

4 Measure 5-ml water into four test-tubes.

5 Put a level spatulaful (or saltspoonful) of ascorbic acid into one test-tube. Cork it and shake it until the crystals dissolve.

6 Add another level spatulaful. Shake the test-tube again. Continue doing this until no more will dissolve, however long you shake. Record the number of level spatulafuls dissolved.

7 Repeat instructions *5* and *6* for citric acid, salt, and sugar.

8 Label these four solutions and keep for use later.

9 Repeat instructions *5* and *6* using approximately 5 ml cooking oil in the fifth test-tube instead of water. Record the solubility of ascorbic acid in oil.

10 Dip a pH indicator paper into each of the four water solutions. Read the pH value from the colour chart.

11 Using the glass rod, add *one* drop of the water solution of ascorbic acid to a blue DCPIP test paper. Note any colour change. Repeat with each of the other water solutions. Clean the glass rod between each test.

12 Fill the dropper with iodine solution. Add three or four drops to each of the four test-tubes containing water solutions. In each case note what happens to the colour of the iodine.

13 In the comments column, compare the results for the four test substances, noting similarities and differences.

Q 5
Vitamins are often classified into two groups, water-soluble and oil-soluble. In which group does vitamin C belong?

Q 6
What was the point of testing citric acid, salt, and sugar when trying to find out the properties of ascorbic acid?

Q 7
Each chemical substance has a unique set of physical and chemical properties which establishes its identity.
a What set of properties have you found so far for ascorbic acid?
b Which are physical and which chemical?

12.3
WHERE IS VITAMIN C FOUND?
If you look at the vitamin C column of the food tables (worksheet M21) you will notice that many foods contain no vitamin C at all. You will find that nearly all the vitamin C in your diet comes from fruit and vegetables.

Figure 12.5
Fresh fruit and vegetables
a *in the Punjab, India*
b *in London.*

Figure 12.6
Potatoes stored in field clamps.

Q 8
a Which two animal foods supply some vitamin C?
b Neither of these is rated as an important source for most people. Why not?

The content of vitamin C in different fruits and vegetables varies greatly. It also changes during storage and processing.

Use the food tables (worksheet M21) together with tables 12.1 and 12.2 to answer the following questions.

Q 9
How good is the advice, 'eat fresh fruit for vitamin C'? Answer with reference to the relative vitamin C content of the items in a fruit bowl in
a mid-winter
b mid-summer.

Figure 12.7
Food label from food fortified with synthetic ascorbic acid.

Storage time	Vitamin C content, mg per 100 g edible weight
Newly dug	30
1 to 3 months	20
4 to 5 months	15
6 to 7 months	10
8 to 9 months	8

Table 12.1
The effect of storage time on the vitamin C content of potatoes.

	Percentage of total national intake supplied by potatoes
Carbohydrates	10.0
Protein	3.6
Fat	0
Ascorbic acid	24.0
Thiamin	9.7
Iron	6.7
Energy	5.0

Table 12.2
The contribution of fresh potatoes to United Kingdom dietary intakes.

Q 10
a What does the information in table 12.2 tell you about the importance of potatoes in the average United Kingdom diet?
b Is this different from the popular 'image' of potatoes?

Q 11
What effect does cooking appear to have on the vitamin C content of foods?

Q 12
Cooking usually results in a 50 per cent loss of vitamin C from Brussels sprouts but only a 30 per cent loss from blackcurrants. Suggest a reason for this.

Q 13
Which method of food preservation would appear to destroy all vitamin C? State the evidence for your answer.

Q 14
Find some evidence to show that not all methods of food preservation destroy vitamin C completely.

In addition to naturally occurring vitamin C, some foods are fortified with synthetic ascorbic acid.

Q 15
In the food tables (worksheet M21e), why is there no numerical value for the vitamin C content of orange squash?

12.4
FINDING OUT FOR YOURSELF

Food composition tables are compiled from results obtained by experts in food analysis. The data in them is very useful — but they only give average, not exact values for particular samples of foods. There are many variables which affect the amount of vitamin C in a food — growing conditions, storage times, cooking and preservation methods. The way to check on your own supplies of vitamin C is to do your own food analysis. The methods suggested on worksheet NM15 depend on one or other of the chemical changes which you observed in section 12.2. Look at your results table.

Q 16
a What was similar about the reactions between vitamin C and both DCPIP and iodine?
b How could you tell they were taking place?

Both reactions can be used to *detect* vitamin C because no other substance present *naturally* in foods will decolorize DCPIP and iodine immediately. Some food preservatives (sulphites and sulphur dioxide) will give the same reaction as vitamin C and could interfere with the test.

Q 17
How could you check whether a packaged food contained sulphites or sulphur dioxide?

The DCPIP test for detecting vitamin C is described on worksheet M19d. If you are not already familiar with the test, try it out on a selection of scraps of food: plant and animal, cooked and raw, fresh and preserved — but only after looking at the label!

Detecting which nutrients are present in a food is called *qualitative analysis*. Measuring amounts of nutrients in foods is called *quantitative analysis*. This involves weighing samples of food for analysis and measuring volumes of reagents of known concentrations. The accuracy of results will depend on the accuracy of the instruments available for weighing and measuring, as well as the skill of the experimenter.

Worksheet NM15 gives you some quick and easy methods which use readily available equipment. The results should be sufficiently accurate to allow useful comparisons to be made. Begin with fruit juices with vitamin C already in solution before tackling foods from which vitamin C has to be washed out.

12.5
LEACHING OUT OF VITAMIN C

Q 18
Look at table 12.3
a Which would appear to be better sources of vitamin C, boiled potatoes or chips? Suggest an explanation.

b Are all chips better sources than all boiled potatoes?

Preparation and cooking method	Vitamin C retained (%)
Peeled and boiled	50 to 70
Peeled, chipped, and deep fried in fat	65 to 75

Table 12.3
The effect of cooking on the ascorbic acid content of potatoes.

Loss of nutrients into water during soaking or boiling is called *leaching out*. Nutrients will not escape from raw vegetables when their outer surfaces are intact. Cutting through cells allows soluble nutrients to pass out into the surrounding water. Cooking makes cell walls porous so that some leaching out is bound to take place from vegetables during boiling.

Q 19
a What is likely to happen if chips are prepared early in the day and left to soak until it is time to cook the dinner?
b How could you check your answer?

Q 20
a Should leaves of cabbage be washed before or after shredding?
b Why is this?

Does the amount of water in which a vegetable is boiled affect the amount of vitamin C leached out? Find out for yourself using an adaptation of the method on worksheet NM15.

Figure 12.8
Methods of cooking affect vitamin C content.

‖ YOU WILL NEED: ‖‖

50 g cauliflower florets
Water
Labels
DCPIP (blue dye) solution
Dilute ethanoic acid

Balance
Vegetable knife
2 small saucepans with lids, marked A and B

Graduated measuring jug, 500-ml
2 graduated beakers, with 100-ml level
Fork
Small conical flask
2 10-ml graduated syringes
Access to cooker

1 Divide 50 g of cauliflower into two equal samples by cutting through each floret. Check that the two samples are equal in weight (25 g each).

2 Measure 100 ml water into pan A and 500 ml water into pan B. Bring both to the boil and add 25 g cauliflower to each.

3 Boil both samples, with pan lids on, for equal lengths of time, until just cooked (7—10 minutes).

Caution: take care that the pan with the very small amount of water does not boil dry.

4 Drain both pans. Put each sample into a graduated beaker containing 50 ml ethanoic acid. Label the beakers A and B.

5 Use a fork to mash the samples of cooked cauliflower thoroughly. Add water to each beaker up to the 100 ml mark. Stir with the fork, then allow to settle.

	Volume of DCPIP to react with 10-ml extract V (mL)	Weight of vitamin C in 10-ml extract $V \times 0.1$ (mg)	Weight of vitamin C in sample $V \times 0.1 \times 10$ (mg)	Weight of vitamin C in 25g raw cauliflower W (mg)	Vitamin C lost during cooking $W-(V \times 0.1 \times 10)$ (mg)
Sample A (small volume of cooking water)				15	
Sample B (large volume of cooking water)				15	

Figure 12.10

6 Using one of the 10-ml graduated syringes, transfer a 10-ml portion of the solution from beaker A to the conical flask. Avoid getting solid bits of cauliflower into the syringe.

7 Fill the other graduated syringe with DCPIP solution and add it, *1 ml at a time*, to the cauliflower extract in the conical flask. Record the number of millilitres of DCPIP used. (See worksheet NM15 for advice on using graduated syringes.)

8 Watch the colour disappear as the solutions mix. Continue, until a pale pink colour lasts for at least 15 seconds.

9 Rinse out the conical flask. Repeat instructions *6, 7,* and *8* above, working quickly until the pale-pink end point is near. Then add DCPIP solution drop by drop, to get a more accurate result. Read the volume used to the nearest whole millilitre. If you are not sure that your result is accurate, do it over again.

Caution: The pale pink colour will fade if left standing. The correct result is the *first* pale pink colour which lasts while you count up to fifteen.

10 Rinse out the conical flask and repeat instructions *6, 7, 8,* and *9* using cauliflower extract from graduated beaker B. Record results in a table like figure 12.10.

11 Calculate the vitamin C lost during cooking by method A and method B.

Q 21
a How did your results differ?
b Is there sufficient difference to make you careful about the amount of water you use when cooking cauliflower or other vegetables which are important sources of vitamin C?

Q 22
In carrying out the experiment, what was done to make sure that different results could be linked to different volumes of cooking water?

12.6
OXIDATION OF VITAMIN C
When you drained the water from the cauliflower you probably threw it away. If you had kept it, you could have tested it to

Figure 12.9

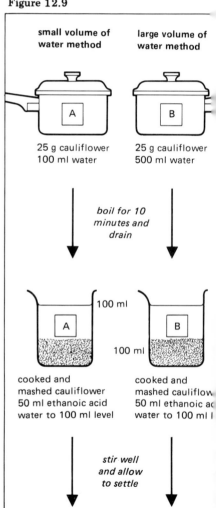

small volume of water method   large volume of water method

A   B

25 g cauliflower 100 ml water   25 g cauliflower 500 ml water

boil for 10 minutes and drain

100 ml

A   B

100 ml

cooked and mashed cauliflower 50 ml ethanoic acid water to 100 ml level   cooked and mashed cauliflow 50 ml ethanoic ac water to 100 ml l

stir well and allow to settle

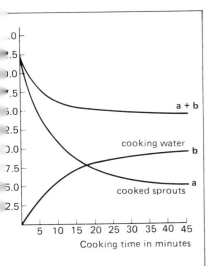

Figure 12.11
Levels of vitamin C in Brussels sprouts and cooking water.

Cooking time in minutes

a + b
cooking water — b
cooked sprouts — a

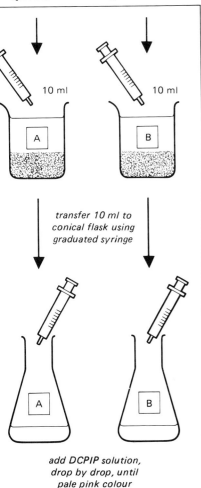

10 ml   10 ml

A   B

transfer 10 ml to
conical flask using
graduated syringe

A   B

add DCPIP solution,
drop by drop, until
pale pink colour
lasts 15 seconds

find how much vitamin C it contained and whether it would be worth using to make gravy. Figure 12.11 shows graphs drawn from some results obtained by cooking sprouts for different lengths of time and measuring the vitamin C in the cooked sprouts and in the cooking water. Here are details of the test.

A 500-g sample of Brussels sprouts was trimmed, halved, and divided into random 25-g samples. Ten boiling-tubes containing 50 ml water were heated in a boiling water-bath to constant maximum temperature. A 25-g sample of sprouts was placed in each boiling-tube. Timing started when maximum temperature was again reached. A boiling-tube was removed from the water-bath for analysis of content at five-minute intervals up to 25 minutes and at ten-minute intervals up to 45 minutes. Any effects due to evaporation of cooking water were ignored.

Q 23
How true is it that the longer Brussels sprouts are boiled, the less vitamin C they contain?

Q 24
a What is the point of the 'a + b' line on the graph?
b Suggest a reason why the vitamin C in Brussels sprouts plus the vitamin C in the cooking water is less than that in the original raw Brussels sprouts.

Ascorbic acid is a reactive chemical and can easily be oxidized. You watched this happening when, in section 12.1, you added DCPIP and iodine to the ascorbic acid solution and saw the immediate colour changes. Unless this oxidation is checked, useful ascorbic acid is changed into a nutritionally useless compound. You have probably heard about vitamin C being 'destroyed'. This was happening to some of the vitamin C in sprouts during cooking. This is the reason why there was less vitamin C in cooked sprouts and cooking water together than in the raw sprouts.

Conditions which favour the oxidation of vitamin C include:

exposure to air (providing oxygen available for oxidation);
presence of oxidizing agents (*i.e.* other chemicals like iron(III) and copper(II) ions, DCPIP, and iodine);
water (chemicals react more quickly when dissolved);
heat (speeds up most chemical changes);
exposure to light (light can provide energy for chemical changes);
alkaline conditions (pH of solution above 7).

Q 25
How could you try to prevent oxidation of vitamin C? Suggest how to reverse each of the conditions above. (Clue: the opposite of an oxidizing agent is a reducing agent.)

Q 26
Why are extracts for vitamin C analysis prepared in acid solutions?

By far the most important cause of oxidation of vitamin C (and therefore of vitamin C destruction) is an enzyme called ascorbic acid oxidase. This is present in plant cells together with vitamin

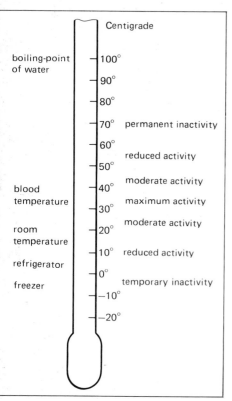

Centigrade

- 100° boiling-point of water
- 90°
- 80°
- 70° permanent inactivity
- 60°
- 50° reduced activity
- 40° moderate activity — blood temperature
- 30° maximum activity
- 20° moderate activity — room temperature
- 10° reduced activity — refrigerator
- 0° — freezer
- −10° temporary inactivity
- −20°

Figure 12.12
Effect of temperature on the activity of ascorbic acid oxidase.

Figure 12.13

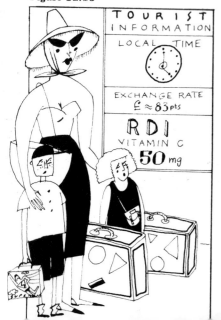

TOURIST
INFORMATION
LOCAL TIME
EXCHANGE RATE
£ ≈ 83 pts
RDI
VITAMIN C
50 mg

C but remains inactive until plant cells are damaged. This happens when crops are harvested and during food preparation and cooking. Ascorbic acid oxidase is most active at warm temperatures, inactive at low temperatures, and destroyed at high temperatures. (See worksheet FSM 18b.)

Q 27
With vitamin C in mind, give reasons for the following:
a using green vegetables as soon as possible after gathering
b handling soft fruits and salad vegetables carefully to prevent bruising
c plunging green vegetables into boiling water at the start of cooking
d blanching fruits and vegetables prior to freezing
e choosing properly stored frozen vegetables in preference to wilting and discoloured 'fresh' vegetables.

12.7
HOW MUCH VITAMIN C DO WE NEED?
Look at the daily allowances of vitamin C recommended by the governments of different countries (table 12.4).

Table 12.4

	Babies	Pregnant and lactating women	Average for moderately active men
United Kingdom	20	60	30
Australia	30	60	30
Norway	15	60	30
West Germany	35	65	45
Holland	30	100	50
India	30	80	50
Japan	35	90	50
United States	35	100	60
France	35	100	75
Switzerland	75*	75*	75*
U.S.S.R.	75	200	100
United Nations (F.A.O.)	20	30	30

*Average for whole population

Does this indicate that the part of the World in which you live determines how much vitamin C you need? Obviously not — it indicates disagreement between the experts who advise on the recommendations.

All experts agree that the diet must provide enough vitamin C to prevent scurvy; but some believe that for positive health the tissues ought be kept saturated with vitamin C. Experiments have shown that as little as 10 mg vitamin C per day is probably enough to prevent scurvy for most people. The United Kingdom government bases its recommendations on this evidence — with 'margins of safety' to cover individual differences and the extra vitamin C needed during illness, injury, and other forms of stress. To saturate our bodies with vitamin C would require intakes averaging at least 60 mg per day.

Q 28
Which governments would appear to base their recommendations on the intakes needed for tissue saturation?

In its Report No 120 called *Recommended intakes of nutrients for the United Kingdom*, the D.H.S.S. states, 'There is, so far, no evidence that Man derives any benefit from such a high intake (60 mg per day for tissue saturation) of ascorbic acid'.

Q 29
a What benefits from high intakes are being claimed by researchers?
b What sort of evidence do you think the D.H.S.S. would find convincing? (This is a difficult question. Jot down your first thoughts, then either discuss in class or take time to find out more about it.)

Q 30
Some people, including certain medical authorities, are already increasing their intakes of vitamin C, believing that it can't do harm and it might do good. What would you expect to happen to extra vitamin C in the body so that it does no harm?

Q 31
If you decide to double your vitamin C intake, what general changes would you make in your diet?

Q 32
Why might the advice to cut down average intakes of fats and sugar and to increase average intakes of dietary fibre lead to improved intakes of vitamin C?

Vitamin C can be stored by the body to a limited extent. Summer treats like strawberries can 'top up' these stores; so can winter oranges.

Q 33
a How has the food processing industry helped to ensure year-round supplies of vitamin C?
b How has the pharmaceutical industry helped to ensure vitamin C supplies.

12.8
IS SCURVY STILL A PROBLEM?
Scurvy is now a rare disease throughout the World. In Britain, the rare cases of obvious scurvy are mainly among elderly people living alone (mainly men). Diets restricted to a few foods and excluding fruits and vegetables are the cause. A few cases of infantile scurvy are reported. Invariably these result from serious neglect by the parents or complete ignorance of how babies should be fed.

Q 34
What services are available which aim to reduce further the cases of scurvy in Britain?

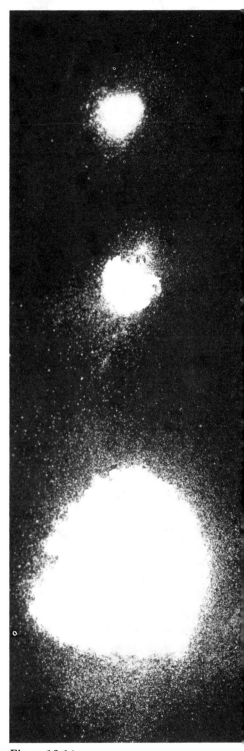

Figure 12.14
Vitamin C (ascorbic acid). 30 mg (United Kingdom R.D.I.), 60 mg (United States R.D.I.), and 4000 mg (huge daily dose suggested, but not proved, as a cold cure).

THE SCOURGE OF THE SEA

In 1497, the explorer, Vasco Da Gama, set out from Portugal to find a trading route to India. On the long voyage, 100 men died from scurvy out of a crew of 160. Over the next three hundred years, the success of long sea trips, whether trade, military, or exploratory, depended a great deal on how much scurvy broke out. Everyone had come to expect outbreaks of the illness on long sea journeys. It was many years before the cause was found.

In 1747, a Scottish naval surgeon called James Lind carried out a famous experiment on board his ship *The Salisbury*. Twelve of the crew had gone down with scurvy. According to Lind, 'they all in general had putrid gums, the spots, and lassitude with weakness of their knees'. Lind gave each patient the same basic diet. He divided them into six pairs and gave each pair one of the following supplements to their diet: a quart of cider per day; elixir vitriol three times a day; two spoonsful of vinegar three times a day; a course of sea water, two oranges, and a lemon per day; and nutmeg with a mixture of mustard, garlic seed, and gum myrrh. The most striking effect was seen in the pair on oranges and lemons — both were fit for duty after six days.

Even though Lind published a paper of his findings in 1753, the British navy did not make it compulsory to carry citrus fruit aboard ships until 1795. So why did Lind's ideas take so long to catch on? One possible reason was that medicine had not come across the idea of a deficiency disease before, and, like most new ideas, it met a lot of resistance. Another reason could have been that no one was prepared to listen to a lowly ship's surgeon. Lind wasn't even a commissioned officer. In those days crew members thought so little of these surgeons that they were laughingly nicknamed 'sawbones'. It was fairly common for the sick to suffer their illness than risk treatment at the hands of one of these doctors.

It was finally the pioneering work of Captain James Cook which convinced the British Admiralty of the value of Lind's work. On joining the Royal Navy, this great explorer was shocked at the amount of scurvy he saw. He was determined that his own crew would remain healthy. His journey aboard the *H.M.S. Endeavour* charted much of the Pacific for the first time. Yet, on his 30 000 mile journey, which took three years, Cook could boast that no one had died from scurvy. On the voyage, Cook insisted on a strict diet for his (often reluctant) crew. The diet always included citrus fruit. He also insisted on clean dry clothing and properly ventilated sleeping quarters. A few disobedient crew members were actually flogged.

It was the start of the Napoleonic wars when Lind's ideas were finally put into practice by the Royal Navy. Eliminating the scourge of scurvy probably doubled Britain's fighting force.

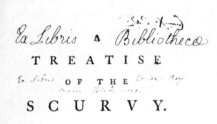

Figure 12.15
Cover of Lind's treatise on scurvy published in 1753.

CHAPTER 13

Carrots, eyes, and vitamin A

13.1
COLOURFUL FOODS

Look at figure 13.1. What have all these foods in common? The question really isn't fair without a colour photograph because the answer wanted is that the foods are highly coloured. This adds to the attractiveness of food. The natural colours of foods are due to *pigments*. These can contribute to the diet by stimulating appetite. One group of pigments — the *carotenes* — are valuable nutrients as well. All the carotenes are yellow/orange or orange/red in colour. All the foods in figure 13.1 contain carotenes. Some contain other pigments as well.

Q 1
a Which foods in figure 13.1 do you think contain other pigments as well as carotenes?
b Name any other pigments you know about already.

Carotenes are named after carrots, a well-known rich source. You can learn about carotenes by looking at them in carrot tissue with a microscope or by extracting them from carrots.

LOOKING FOR CAROTENES

||| YOU WILL NEED: |||||||||||||||||||||||||||||||||||||||||||||||||||||||||||||||||||||||||||||||

Small piece of raw carrot

Microscope
Clean slide and coverslip

Sharp vegetable knife
Mounted needle
Worksheet M27

1 Cut a very thin section through the carrot. Some practice may be needed to obtain one wafer-thin slice. Spread it out in the middle of the slide.

2 Add a drop of water and lower the coverslip using the mounted needle (see worksheet M27).

3 Record the colour of the carrot as seen with the naked eye.

4 Focus with low power and search the carrot section for a part thin enough to allow separate cells to be seen (the edge of the section may be the thinnest part). Note the colour.

5 Continue searching in order to find solid particles, angular in shape (sometimes star-shaped), and dark orange in colour. These are chromoplasts made of crystalline carotene.

6 Change to high power and examine one chloroplast carefully. Draw what you see and label the cell walls and chromoplasts.

Figure 13.1
Colourful foods.

Q 2

What does this tell you about carotene solubility in water? (Remember that the cell sap surrounding these chromoplasts is mainly water.)

EXTRACTING CAROTENES

||| **YOU WILL NEED:** ||||||||||||||||||||||||||||||||||||||||||||||||||||||||||||||||||||||||||||||||||||||||||||||||||||||||||||||||||||

½ medium-sized carrot	Small saucepan with lid
Water	Hotplate
Cooking oil	2 similar shallow white dishes
	Frying spatula
Vegetable knife	

Figure 13.2

water drained from par-boiled carrots

pour off the oil into the second dish

1 Slice the carrot thinly and put into the saucepan.

2 Add just enough water to cover the carrot and heat to boiling.

3 Reduce the heat and simmer for 10 minutes, with the lid on.

4 Strain the cooking water into one of the white dishes, keeping the carrot slices in the pan.

5 Add just enough cooking oil to cover the carrot slices and return the pan to the hotplate.

6 *Gently* heat the carrots in the oil for 10 minutes, stirring frequently. Replace the lid between stirrings.

7 Remove the pan from the hotplate and pour off the cooking oil into the second white dish.

8 Note the colour of both the water extract and the oil extract.

Q 3

Which solvent, water or oil, would appear better at extracting carotene?

13.2
CAROTENE AND VITAMIN A

Carotene is important in the diet because after it is absorbed some of it is converted into vitamin A. Carotene occurs as a pigment in fruits and vegetables. A few animal foods contain both vitamin A and carotene.

Q 4

Name two animal foods which contain both vitamin A and carotene. (Clue: look again at figure 13.1.)

The conversion of carotene into vitamin A in the body is not very efficient. To begin with, it is not easily absorbed because of its insolubility in water. (Remember those solid particles called chromoplasts seen under the microscope.) The addition of fat to fruits and vegetables will help to dissolve the carotene which can then be absorbed as an emulsion.

After absorption, the splitting of molecules of carotene to give vitamin A is not complete. Unchanged carotene molecules can remain in the tissues. When calculations of carotene intakes are being made, in order to allow for limited absorption and splitting, weights of carotene in the diet have to be divided by 6 before

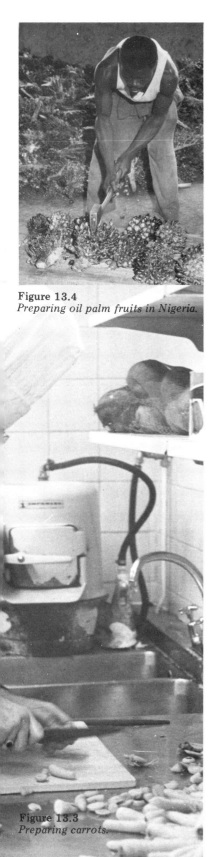

Figure 13.4
Preparing oil palm fruits in Nigeria.

Figure 13.3
Preparing carrots.

being added to weights of vitamin A. This has been done for you in the food tables on worksheet M21. Note that there is just one column headed 'Vitamin A, μg'.

If you needed to know the vitamin A content of a food not in your own food tables, you would look in reference books such as McCance and Widdowson's *Composition of foods* or Platt's *Values of foods commonly used in tropical countries*. These give separate information for retinol (the chemical name for vitamin A) and for carotene. The calculation below shows the allowance for the limited absorption and conversion of carotene in adding up the total vitamin A value of 100 g shredded suet.

	retinol, μg	carotene, μg
suet, shredded	52	73

The retinol equivalent of 73 μg carotene = $\frac{73}{6}$ = 12 μg.

Total vitamin A value of 100 g shredded suet = 52 + 12 = 64 μg.

Q 5
Red palm oil is an important source of vitamin A in some African countries. Its carotene content is very high: 30 000 μg carotene per 100 g. What is its vitamin A equivalent per 100 g?

Q 6
Cod-liver oil contains retinol, not carotene. Its content is 18 000 μg retinol per 100 g. How does it compare with red palm oil for vitamin A?

Cod-liver oil is not normally included in United Kingdom diets. Its use is only medicinal, as a vitamin supplement.

Q 7
a Search your food tables for a food which comes near to cod-liver oil for vitamin A value. Remember to adjust weights for portion sizes to weights per 100 g.
b What other nutrients is this food important for?

Q 8
a Look again at your food tables and find the second richest source of vitamin A – a vegetable this time. Give the vitamin A value per 100 g.
b Do you think that the method of cooking this vegetable could affect its contribution to the body's supply of vitamin A? Refer to your results from experiments in section 13.1 and to familiar uses of this vegetable.

When you were using your food tables to find answers to questions 7 and 8, you probably noticed how few animal foods contain vitamin A. Milk and eggs are sources of vitamin A.

Q 9
Why could you have guessed that milk and eggs would contain vitamin A?

Q 10
a Why is the vitamin A in the yolk and not in the white of eggs?
b Why is there more vitamin A in cream cheese than in cottage cheese?

115

Water-insoluble vitamin A molecules can only be carried in blood when attached to other water-soluble molecules. A special protein (called retinol-binding protein) provides these molecules which can carry vitamin A. Any vitamin A in excess of the body's needs is carried to the liver for storage. The kidneys also store small amounts.

13.3
WHY DOES THE BODY NEED VITAMIN A?

In 1912, Frederick Gowland Hopkins carried out some research on rats which led to the discovery that vitamin A plays a part in growth. Vitamin A is also involved in dim-light vision. Find out how good your dim-light vision is. Divide the class into two groups: one group to be tested (the subjects), the other to prepare and carry out the test (the operators).

IIII YOU WILL NEED: IIIIIIIIIIIIIIIIIIIIIIIIIIIIIIIIIIIIIIIIIIIIIIIIIIIIIIIIIIIIIIIIIIIIIIIIIIIIIIIIIIIIIIIIIIIIIII

Room with black-out curtains or blinds
Table in the centre of the room
Semicircle of chairs, one for each of the subjects and each 10 paces away from the table
Stopwatch for each of the subjects
5 or 6 similar-shaped objects to be placed on the table for identification, *e.g.* spherical objects, like balls and fruit, or rectangular solids, like packets — if possible in different bright colours

Instructions to the subjects
1 Leave the room while the operators prepare the test.

2 Look at the sky so that enough light is reaching your eye retina to use up the vision pigments. Do not look at the sun — if the sun is shining, turn your back on it and look at the sky. ⚠

Instructions to the operators
3 Choose the objects, unknown to the subjects, and put them on the table. Arrange the chairs, draw the blinds, and put out the lights.

4 Tell the subjects to close their eyes (or use blind-folds) and lead them to a chair in the room.

5 Give each subject a stop watch and tell them to start it as they open their eyes and try to identify the objects.

Instructions to the subjects
6 As soon as you are sure you can identify the objects on the table stop the watch. Try to make out the colour as well as the identity of the objects.

Instructions to all
7 When all subjects have adjusted to dim-light vision, the light should be turned on and the stopwatches read so that the times taken can be compared.

Q 11
Why could the objects not be seen on entering the darkened room?

Figure 13.5
Seeing in the dark.

Q 12

What happened in the retina rods during the few minutes of adjustment to dim-light vision?

Q 13

Why might some subjects adjust more quickly than others?

Q 14

Were your colour-sensitive cones able to function in the dim light?

13.4
HOW MUCH IS ENOUGH?

How much vitamin A are you getting and is it enough?

Make a quick estimate of your likely intake of vitamin A for *one* day. Use your selection of food portions sufficient for your day's meals made in Chapter 8.

IIII YOU WILL NEED: IIIIIIIIIIIIIIIIIIIIIIIIIIIIIIIIIIIIIIIIIIIIIIIIIIIIIIIIIIIIIIIIIIIIIIIIIIIIIIIIIIIIIIIIIIIIIII
Completed results table (*figure 8.2*)
Worksheet M21 (food tables)
Worksheet M18b (recommended daily intakes)

1 Check back to Chapter 8 to remind yourself of the class decisions recorded in columns 1, 2, and 3 and your own decisions about completing columns 4 and 5.

2 Call the blank column 6 'Vitamin A (μg)' and use the food tables to fill in the weights of vitamin A in your chosen portions.

3 Find the day's total and compare it with the recommended daily intake of vitamin A for your group, as shown on worksheet M18b.

Q 15

Is your day's total above or below the recommendation for your group?

The chances are that if you happen to have chosen liver or carrots, your total will be well above the recommendation. On the other hand, if it was a day when you had cauliflower rather than cabbage, meat or fish rather than eggs and cheese, and apples rather than oranges, your vitamin A intake could be well below. Does this matter? Probably not, because we can store enough vitamin A in our livers to last for many months without any additional intakes.

Having 'enough' means showing no symptoms of deficiency. Tests for impaired dim-light vision, similar to your investigation in section 13.3, give early signs. Confirming such early signs involves taking a blood sample and measuring the concentration of vitamin A in the blood plasma.

At present there is little cause for concern about this in Britain. Even so, no changes should be made in diets without thinking about how they would effect vitamin A intakes.

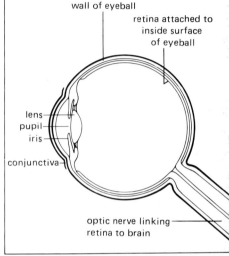

Figure 13.6
The human eye.

Figure 13.7

Q 16
Why was fortification of margarine with vitamin A introduced during the Second World War?

Q 17
How would changing to a lacto-vegetarian diet affect vitamin A intakes?

Q 18
What advice would be helpful to someone changing to a vegan diet? Remember methods of cooking and serving foods could be important as well as the choice of rich sources of vitamin A.

Q 19
How might the changes urged by the dietary guidelines affect vitamin A intakes?

13.5
THE INTERNATIONAL SITUATION
Figure 13.8 shows how much more dependent the developing countries are on carotene than those in the West. Carotene ought to be abundant in developing countries and yet blinding malnutrition is widespread due to vitamin A deficiency.

It is a tragic problem, with half a million new cases reported annually. Bangladesh, India, Indonesia, and the Philippines are worst affected, followed by many but not all countries in Africa, and also some countries in South and Central America.

Reasons for vitamin A deficiencies in these countries are:

vegetable crops not being available during the dry season of the year;
poor cooking methods (boiling instead of stir-frying);
lack of oil in the diet;
economic pressures to sell produce (mangoes and eggs) for cash;
not giving vegetables to young children either because the children 'do not like them' or in the belief that they cause diarrhoea.

Q 20
Why is boiling considered a poor cooking method and stir-frying a good one? Refer in your answer to your experimental results in section 13.1.

Q 21
Why would more oil in the diet improve the vitamin A status of people living in developing countries?

Q 22
Why are mangoes and eggs singled out as crops which ought not to be sold but kept for home consumption? (Clue: mangoes are fruits with deep yellow-orange flesh.)

Q 23
Can you suggest how to get young children to eat, and enjoy, vegetables?

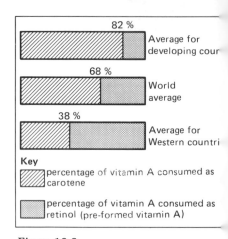

Figure 13.8
Relative dependence on carotene for vitamin A supplies.

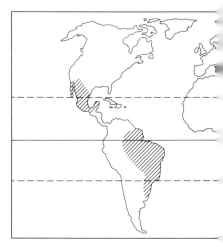

Figure 13.9
Areas of the World where blinding malnutrition is a major problem.

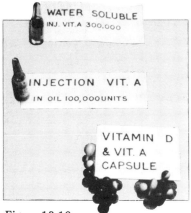

Figure 13.10
Three forms of vitamin A used in the treatment of xerophthalmia. If treated in time, the eyes can by completely cured.

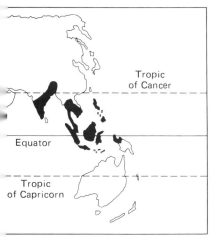

Figure 13.11
Fruits on a market stall with carotene contents ranging from 1500 μg per 100 g in apricots to only traces in white grapes.

Q 24

What is the real cause of diarrhoea among children in poorer communities in tropical countries? (Refer back to Chapter 5.)

Q 25

Suggest a reason why some countries in Africa have better vitamin A intakes than others. (Clue: see figure 13.4.)

Research into the functions of vitamin A in the diet continues. Findings have included links with the prevention of infection and of certain cancers.

BACKGROUND READING

THE TWENTIETH CENTURY PLAGUE

Xerophthalmia (caused by lack of vitamin A) is one of the biggest nutritional problems in the World today. The World Health Organization estimates that lack of vitamin A blinds from twenty thousand to one hundred thousand children every year, and kills an equal number. The worst affected areas seem to be the regions of South East Asia where rice forms the staple diet, though parts of Latin America and Africa are also affected.

Most children with xerophthalmia are fairly easy to treat. If the eye damage hasn't gone too far, an injection of the vitamin into a muscle will reverse the symptoms. But the problem is that if children go back to the same conditions which caused the xerophthalmia in the first place it is just as likely to strike again. Because of this, organizations like UNICEF have helped governments in developing countries to experiment with methods of preventing the illness rather than curing it.

One idea has been to give out massive doses of vitamin A every few months to groups thought to be in danger of the disease. This has been tried in areas such as India, Bangladesh, and Indonesia but, on the whole, the trials have not been successful. The main difficulty seemed to be getting the vitamin to those who need it most — something like 30 per cent of those thought to be in need could not be reached. These were usually refugees, slum dwellers, or the rural poor living miles from any main roads. There was also a high drop-out rate for further doses. In Indonesia, the numbers dropped by 20 per cent each time a new dose had to be given.

Although lack of dietary vitamin A is the main cause of xerophthalmia, there are other factors involved such as protein-energy malnutrition, tuberculosis, diarrhoea, and measles. All these other factors, which normally affect the poor more than any other group, mean that it is not enough simply to raise vitamin A intakes. In the fight against this twentieth-century plague, it is poverty and the conditions resulting from poverty which really need to be tackled.

CHAPTER 14

Who's special?

14.1
NUTRITIONAL NEEDS AND RECOMMENDATIONS

Breast milk is the ideal food for a baby. Later in life many more foods are in your diet, and you can satisfy your nutritional needs from a large variety of them. What you think is a need for food may not be an actual requirement for good health. The nutrients and energy required by the body for good health are called nutritional requirements.

Many factors affect your nutritional requirements, for example, physical activity, your age, sex, size, and health. How much have you already learned about these individual nutritional needs? See if you can answer the following questions.

Q 1
What are the important nutrients in cows' milk which make it a valuable food for children and young people?

Q 2
What do dietary guidelines for the United Kingdom advise about eating fat?

Q 3
Look at worksheet M18b. What could a pregnant woman eat in a day to ensure she is supplied with enough protein?

Q 4
Why is extra calcium recommended during pregnancy?

Q 5
What foods, other than dairy foods, could be eaten to supply the calcium recommended for pregnant women?

Q 6
For a woman with a good diet who becomes pregnant, which are the nutrients she should pay particular attention to?

Q 7
Why should fresh and carefully prepared vegetables be an important feature in the diet of young people?

Q 8
Why is iron particularly important in the diets of women and girls?

Q 9
Why do children require more energy in relation to their body size than adults?

Q 10
Why is egg yolk often given to babies as they are weaned?

Figure 14.1
Size affects nutritional requirements!

Figure 14.2
Eating an egg.

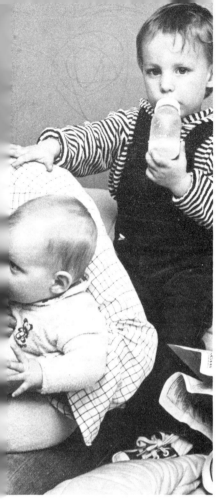

Figure 14.3
Food costs money.

Q 11
Why is it a bad idea to add sugar to a toddler's food?

Baked beans are recommended to people who want a high-fibre diet.

Q 12
a Why is this?
b What are their disadvantages, and how can they be overcome?

Q 13
What is the most important factor in an athlete's diet?

It is important to remember that you do not eat nutrients — you eat foods which supply nutrients. The body must be supplied with nutrients from foods which are readily available, are acceptable, and are within the purchasing power of the buyer.

14.2
FOOD COSTS MONEY

Economic considerations play a part in determining what we choose to eat. Food manufacturers do a great deal of research into how they price their products. The relationship between choice and price is not always a simple one, though usually more of a food is bought when it goes down in price. The increase in the consumption of chicken over the past twenty years is mainly due to its decrease in price.

Most families try to spend the same amount on food every week. It is quite possible to have a good diet for far less than some families spend. There is no direct connection between the cost of a food and its nutritional value, but it is true that some cheap foods need careful and imaginative cooking.

Q 14
Give *two* examples of such foods.

Q 15
List *three* separate points you would give as advice on how to avoid overspending on food.

Q 16
a Comment on the cost and nutritional value of the menu below.
b Suggest cheaper alternatives to make a similar meal to as many of the foods as you can.

Cream of chicken soup
Salmon mousse
Rump steak with frozen peas, chips, mushrooms, and tomatoes
Black Forest gateau
Lymeswold or Brie cheese

14.3
DO WE ALL EAT THE SAME FOODS?

What people eat differs according to regional and cultural variations, religious and moral beliefs, as well, of course, as personal likes and dislikes. People in the same region are often a mixture of different cultures and religions. When investigating people's eating habits, it must be remembered that a satisfactory and enjoyable diet can be achieved in a variety of ways.

What elderly people eat may be influenced by the following factors:

medication which interferes with the absorption of nutrients;
food choice limited by their income;
housebound and unable to shop;
living and eating alone;
small appetite due to lack of physical activity;
dentures or poor teeth which make it difficult to chew;
disabilities, such as arthritis, which make preparing food difficult;
unfamiliarity with new food products.

Figure 14.4
Salad Nicoise is enjoyed by vegetarians who eat fish and eggs.

Figure 14.5
Vegan salad

Q 17
From your knowledge of the food choices of other groups, make a list of factors which may influence eating patterns.

Some people will not eat animal foods because they are *vegetarians.* Those vegetarians who will not eat meat, fish, cheese, eggs, or milk are known as *vegans.* Others who will not eat meat or fish, but will eat dairy foods, are called *lacto-vegetarians.*

Why do you think people become vegetarians? There are many different reasons. Discuss it, if you can, with someone who is a vegetarian.

How can nutritional requirements be met within different feeding patterns? A closer investigation of vegan diets will show how this can be done for one group of people.

For vegans, the foods in figure 14.5 form the basis of the diet.

Figure 14.6
a *Normal small intestine. Healthy villi form a large surface area for the absorption of food.*

Q 18
a If no dairy foods (eggs, milk, and cheese) and no flesh foods (meat and fish) are eaten, which foods would supply protein in the diet?
b Why are mixtures of different plant proteins especially important in the diets of vegans? (See Chapter 9 for clues.)

Q 19
a If protein needs are met from the foods listed in your answer to question 18a, what other nutrients, normally associated with animal sources of protein, may still be lacking?
b Which other foods could be eaten to provide these nutrients?

This example shows the wide variety of foods which can be chosen to meet nutritional requirements.

14.4
SPECIAL DIETS

Some people need medical advice on what they should eat because they have *metabolic* problems. This means that their bodies are unable to metabolize (use effectively) some of the important nutrients. Once diagnosed, many of these disorders can be treated, but they involve a special diet.

Q 20
Make a list of the disorders you have heard about in which the diet plays a part.

One example of a metabolic disorder which can only be controlled by the person following a special diet is *coeliac disease*. A person with coeliac disease cannot tolerate *gluten*.

Q 21
a   What is gluten?
b   Which foods contain gluten?

Imagine how difficult it is not to eat any gluten at all. List all the foods that you have eaten today that contained gluten.

Look at figure 14.6, and answer the following question.

Q 22
What differences do you notice between the sections of intestine shown in figures 14.6a and b?

In Chapter 4 you learned about protein digestion and absorption. You learned how the diet provides the body with the amino acids it needs in Chapter 9. It is thought that coeliac disease involves a deficiency in the intestine of a particular enzyme that splits up the peptides from gluten. When this enzyme is lacking, the peptides are absorbed without being split into amino acids. This causes the cells of the intestine to swell. The disease also interferes with the absorption of fat, carbohydrates, protein, and some vitamins.

Coeliac disease usually occurs in children under three years old. The symptoms are slow growth, lack of appetite, and a pot-belly. The only way to treat them is to exclude completely from their diets wheat flour and wheat products, oats, rye, and all other foods containing gluten. Some products are specially labelled show coeliacs that they are safe (figure 14.7). The Coeliac Society provides help and advice to parents and those suffering from the disease.

Q 23
What is supplied by wheat in the normal diet which will have to be supplied from other sources in a coeliac's diet?

Q 24
Suggest some foods which do not contain gluten which could be used for producing a gluten-free flour for use by coeliacs.

b   *Coeliac small intestine. The lining is completely flat.*

Figure 14.7
The crossed grain symbol on a food packet tells a coeliac that the product is safe.

Another example of a diet-related condition is *diabetes*. This is more common than coeliac disease, and it is equally important that the diet is controlled. Very young people can suffer from diabetes. In later life the disease can develop as a result of lifelong bad eating habits. Diabetics are unable to utilize the sugar in their diets. They therefore excrete it in the urine, which finally results in a breakdown of the urinary tract. Diabetics also find it difficult to keep a healthy weight. They need a diet low in refined carbohydrate (sugar) and sufficiently low in energy to keep their weight appropriate for their age and size. Low-energy diets are likely to be low in fat as well.

Q 25
What other advantages are there in having a diet which is low in fat?

Q 26
Unrefined carbohydrates are important in the diet of a diabetic. How would you recommend such a person to increase their intake of unrefined carbohydrate?

Non-nutritive sweeteners, such as saccharine, can be taken by diabetics.

Q 27
What other advantages are there in reducing the sugar in a diet?

Q 28
What dietary guidelines would you recommend to a person suffering from:
a diabetes
b coeliac disease.

14.5
MEALS FOR INDIVIDUALS
Within a family or group it is rarely possible, or socially acceptable, for each person to eat a different meal. Time and cost also make it difficult. Part of the art of planning meals is using the adaptability of foods to suit all those eating the meal. Try planning a meal for a variety of people.

IIII YOU WILL NEED: IIIIIIIIIIIIIIIIIIIIIIIIIIIIIIIIIIIIIIIIIIIIIIIIIIIIIIIIIIIIIIIIIIIIIIIIIIIIIIIIIIIIIIII

Worksheet M18	Recipe books
Worksheet M21	Pen and paper

1 A list of common dishes and a list of people that might have to be catered for at a meal is given on the next page. Plan a meal choosing four people and suitable dishes from the lists.

2 Adapt recipes for each dish to meet the particular needs of those at your meal so that they can all eat together.

YOURS? AND YOUR

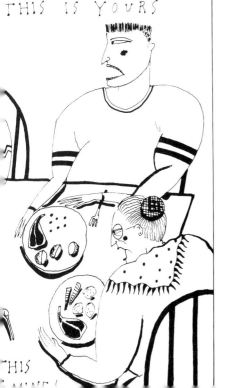
Figure 14.9

Figure 14.8
Diabetic Gary Mabbutt of Tottenham and England can compete at the top level of his sport.

Dishes	For
Soup	Yourself
Burger	Sister, seven months pregnant
Chicken curry	Brother-in-law, an office worker
Lamb casserole	Grandfather, on a low fat diet
Chilli con carne	Mother, on a weight-reducing diet
Pizza	Father, a manual worker
Fish mornay	Brother, five years old
Vegetables, in season	Brother, a vegetarian
Fruit salad and custard	Brother's girlfriend, a vegan
Mousse	Your friend, a diabetic
Cheese and biscuits	
Bread and butter	
Squash, cola, beer, or wine	

3 Calculate the nutrients supplied by the meal and identify those which are not supplied.

Does the meal you have prepared meet the following criteria?

1 Is the meal attractive?
2 Does the meal fulfil the dietary guidelines?
3 Is the meal likely to satisfy the nutritional recommendations for the stated individuals?

If it does not meet these criteria, then explain why not and suggest improvements.

It will be obvious from your own experiences that people eat very different foods from one another and that, on the whole, they stay healthy. People who have a restricted diet, whether this is for health, cultural, or religious reasons, or simply because they dislike or feel that they cannot afford many of the foods which are available, will need to be particularly careful to choose foods which contain the nutrients they need. The best advice is to eat as large a variety of foods as possible, to eat fresh food in season, and to cook with care and imagination.

BACKGROUND READING

FOOD FOR THOUGHT

Man has always hunted and killed animals for food: primitive Man had little choice if he wanted to survive. In modern times, various people have begun to question the need to kill animals. In 1847 one such group formed the British Vegetarian Society. Members of this society took the decision not to eat animal flesh. In their view both the way animals were kept in factory farms and the way they were slaughtered was cruel.

Britain is not alone in having vegetarians. Certain classes of Hindus, the main religious group in India, are encouraged not to eat meat. They believe in *reincarnation*. This means they believe that after death the soul of man or animal can transfer from one life form to another. Because of this, all life is thought to be

125

sacred. Vegetarian groups can also be found amongst the Seventh-day Adventists of America and the Rastafarian movement which originated in Jamaica.

A recent survey of British vegetarians and vegans asked why they had changed their eating habits so dramatically. Most answered that they hated the idea of killing animals for food. Many also said that they had switched after a long period of illness and found that their health had improved. Other felt that in a world where so many people go hungry it was wrong to eat animals, and that more food can be produced by growing plant crops than by raising animals.

The meat eaters amongst us might expect a vegetarian diet to be boring. In fact a trip to a vegetarian restaurant would show that these diets can be as varied and exciting as any other. Even dishes like 'cottage pie' and paella can be made without meat.

Vegetarian diets have often come in for criticism for nutritional reasons. Most of this is unfair. The only nutrients that may be in short supply are vitamins B_{12} and D. These are found mainly in meat and dairy produce. Vegetarians and vegans know about this and take vitamin supplements as a precaution. There is even evidence to show that vegetarians are particularly healthy. They suffer less from heart disease and bowel disorders. This is probably because of their high-fibre, low-fat diets. Vegan diets are often recommended for the treatment of heart disease.

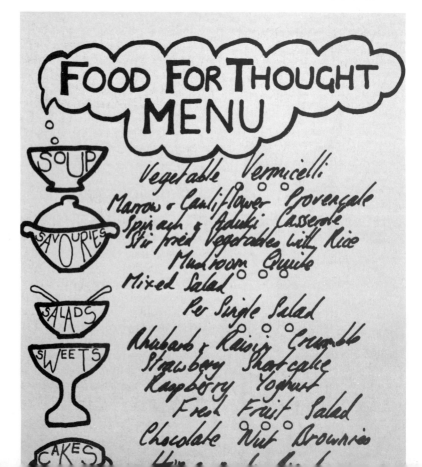

Figure 14.10
Menu from a vegetarian resturant in London.

126

CHAPTER 15

Lessons for the future

15.1
WHO DECIDES WHAT YOU EAT?

How long does it take to satisfy your appetite? Many would answer 'just as long as it takes to open a packet of crisps'. Ready-to-eat snacks and quickly prepared meals are very popular, particularly among young people. They like the freedom which snacks and fast foods give in choosing when, where, and what to eat.

The operation of producing the crisps, to satisfy the demands of consumers like you, begins with the *planning* stage. For example, the manufacturer of crisps arranges matters with farmers who provide the potatoes. The farmers have to decide how much land is required to sow them. Factory space and labour requirements have to be planned.

Figure 15.1

January	February	March	April
Ploughing		Sowing	

May	June	July	August

September	October	November	December
Harvesting			

Figure 15.2
The potato growing year.

127

Q 1
What information would help the manufacturer decide how many packets of potato crisps to produce?

Q 2
Supermarket sales of many packaged foods can be monitored by a special labelling device (figure 15.3). Who is helped by this kind of information?

Carrying out production plans successfully depends on the experience of farmer and manufacturer. The operation must be continually *evaluated*.

Q 3
Suggest how potato crisp producers might set about evaluating their product.

If market research showed that potato crisps were losing their popularity, the manufacturer would start looking for a new variety of snack to attract customers. In fact, manufacturers are always on the look out for ideas — for new flavours or new ways of packaging their products.

Q 4
If you had an idea for a new type of snack, how would you try to persuade a manufacturer to try it?

The stages of manufacture can be summarized as follows.

1 The *planning* stage involves recipe development, test production, and trial marketing.
2 The *implementing* stage is the equipping of the new production line, the training of operatives, and an advertising campaign.

Figure 15.3
Machine readable code on food packaging.

Figure 15.4
Your choice!

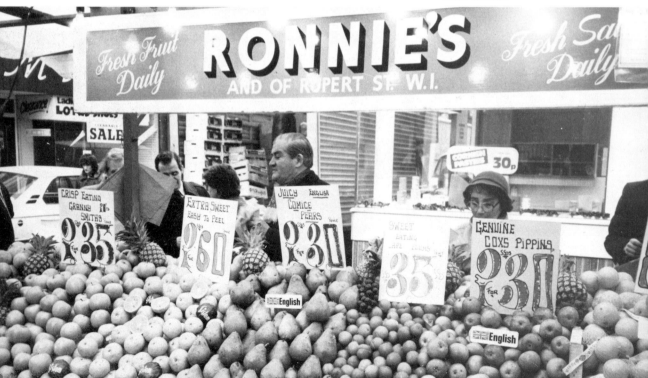

3 The *evaluating* stage involves checking sales figures and providing information for future production levels to be calculated.

You may think that food producers (farmers) and food suppliers (manufacturers and retailers) control what food is available for you' to eat. But it is really you, and other consumers like you, who are in control. It is only food which consumers choose (and pay for) which continues to be available.

Q 5
Make a list of ten snack foods you have eaten. Compare your list with other people's in the class.

15.2
WHY DO FARMERS PRODUCE THE FOODS THEY DO?
In some countries whole families work together on the land. It takes all their labour to produce enough food to feed themselves. This is sometimes not enough to prevent malnutrition. Crops are limited, usually to the local staple. Keeping livestock depends on having grazing land or surplus corn for feedstock.

The labour of a single farmer, in an industrialized country like the United Kingdom, can produce enough to feed a large number of people. Agricultural technology in developed countries is responsible for this high productivity. This type of farming uses a lot of energy to drive machinery and to make fertilizers and crop sprays.

Figure 15.5
Threshing by hand in a village in West Bengal, India.

Figure 15.6
Farming like this needs lots of energy and money.

High technology farming requires a great deal of money to be invested. Farmers expect to get a good return for their money. Crops which can be produced most economically, and for which there is a reliable market, are likely to be chosen. Increasingly, in developed countries, farmers are moving away from forms of farming which need a lot of labour.

Figure 15.7
In the 1940s the consumption of fat was kept low by rationing.

Q 6
a Which are the forms of farming which involve long working hours and a seven-day week?
b Why does this increase production costs?
c Do you think 'factory farming' is the answer to this problem?

Q 7
Why do you think the mid-west of the United States and the prairie states of Canada are called the 'World's bread basket'?

Q 8
What circumstances do you think would favour large-scale beef production?

15.3
WHY DON'T WE RUN OUT OF FOOD?

In the United Kingdom, the government monitors and has a certain amount of control over the food supply. In times of national emergency, such as a war, the government can introduce rationing to make sure that food is properly distributed. In normal times large quantities of food are imported from other countries.

Membership of the Common Market (also known as the European Economic Community or E.E.C.) involves the United Kingdom in trade matters which are frequently debated in Parliament and reported in the newspapers and television.

Q 9

What impression have you gained of the effects which membership of the Common Market has had on food supplies in the United Kingdom?

Public satisfaction with the availability of food is one measure of success. Equally important is a check on the nutritional value of the foods available.

Q 10

How does the government find out about food which is regularly being bought for consumption by households in the United Kingdom?
(Clue: look back to Chapter 1 for information about the N.F.S.)

15.4
CHANGING THE NATIONAL DIET

Economic reasons

Food supplies relate closely to national wealth. The poorer a country, the greater its problems of food shortage and diseases of malnutrition. Present methods of food production in developed countries have been introduced in times of prosperity. If the economic situation in the United Kingdom got worse, food would have to be produced more cheaply.

Worksheet NM18 gives information which shows why meat production is so costly in terms of energy. The problems of increasing food production without wasteful use of natural resources must be solved in order to maintain nutritional standards in the developed countries, and, at the same time, to improve nutritional standards in the less-developed regions of the World.

Health reasons

In earlier chapters references have been made to diet-linked health problems.

Q 11

What health problems can be linked to a diet which includes high levels of:
a sugar
b energy
c fat
d alcohol
e salt?

Q 12

What health problems can be linked to a diet which has low levels of:
a dietary fibre
b vitamin A
c vitamin C
d vitamin D
e absorbable iron?

Figure 15.8

Q 13

Which of the health problems in your answers to questions 12 and 13 only affect clearly identified groups in the United Kingdom?

Q 14

Which problems only occur rarely in the United Kingdom?

Throughout this book references have been made to dietary guidelines in the Department of Health and Social Security's booklet *Eating for health*. The guidelines were aimed to persuade the public to make adjustments to their diets to improve the general level of health. They have been discussed and developed since they were published in 1978 (see the Background reading in Chapter 2).

The health problems which the guidelines tackle are widespread in the United Kingdom population. One of these is coronary heart disease. It is quite normal for elderly people to die from heart disease. During the 1950s and 1960s, a change in statistics about deaths was noticed (see table 15.1).

	England and Wales						Scotland					
Age	35—44		45—54		55—64		35—44		45—54		55—64	
Sex	M	F	M	F	M	F	M	F	M	F	M	F
1950—2	33	8	167	42	566	211	53	18	248	74	755	334
1960—2	53	8	217	39	655	194	75	14	313	73	891	327
1970—2	66	10	274	46	717	194	88	19	355	85	915	317
1979—80	55	9	270	50	718	204	71	13	351	88	901	322

Table 15.1
Annual death rates from coronary heart disease for every 100 000 of the population.

Q 15

a What difference do you notice between the figures for men and women?
b Does this apply to all age groups, at all times, and in both regions?

Medical and nutritional scientists were quick to investigate the possible link between the increase in deaths from coronary heart disease with increased amounts of fat in the diet. Their researches, beginning in the 1950s, were able to supply evidence which set up very lively debates about the effects of the type and amount of fats in the diet on health. The messages which came through the newspapers, radio, and television to the general public during the 1960s were not only that too much fat could be harmful, but that animal fats were more harmful than vegetable oils.

Figure 15.9

Figure 15.10
Margarine 'high in polyunsaturates'.

Such messages are over-simplified. There is scientific evidence linking risks of one type of coronary heart disease to high intakes of saturated fatty acids (SFAs). Other evidence suggests that polyunsaturated fatty acids (PUFAs) can protect against another form of coronary heart disease. All fats contain both SFAs and PUFAs, but butter fat contains more SFAs and less PUFAs than soft ('tub') margarines (see worksheets FSM 5a and NM17). Margarine manufacturers were quick to use this in advertising their products. The dairy industry, concerned about butter sales, was just as quick to point to the weaknesses in the evidence.

There are still a lot of questions to be answered. For example: why is coronary heart disease more common in Scotland than in England and Wales? Why is there such a difference in coronary heart disease rates between the sexes? All medical advisers are very keen to stress that diet is not the only factor which is linked to risks of coronary heart disease. Smoking, lack of exercise, stress, obesity, high blood pressure, and a family history of heart disease all increase the risk.

Were people scared by all the publicity in the 1960s about dangers from fats? Perhaps — certainly fat consumption started to fall (see the graph below).

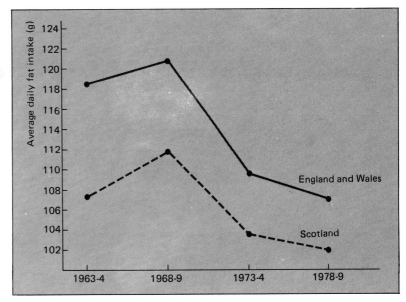

Figure 15.11
Average daily fat intake in England and Wales and Scotland.

Q 16
What happened to the death rate from coronary heart disease? Find the answer from your own graph. Would it be correct to say that the change in death rate in the late 1970s was due to the change in fat intake of the early 1970s?

15.5
PLANNING FOR THE FUTURE

Are we all doing enough to improve or maintain good health by eating wisely? Recent statistics show increased popularity of high-fibre foods and decreased consumption of fat — two changes advocated in dietary guidelines. Decreases in surgical cases of bowel disease and a fall in deaths from coronary heart disease make it look as though these guidelines are pointing in the right direction.

If this is so, then an all-out campaign, with clear statements about healthy eating and advice on how to achieve it, might bring about even greater improvements. To plan such a campaign requires clearly defined objectives and a reasonable time-scale.

To put the plans into practice, effective methods must be worked out and workers given the necessary information and materials. Evaluating the campaign involves measuring its results, and, possibly, reassessing the objectives themselves.

In October 1983, a discussion paper was published by the Health Education Council, called *Proposals for nutritional guidelines for health education in Britain*. It was written by a working party set up by the National Advisory Committee on Nutrition Education (see worksheet NM19).

The proposed nutritional guidelines concentrate on the same health problems as the existing guidelines, but some different approaches are taken. Clear objectives are stated as actual amounts by which consumption of certain nutrients should be increased and others decreased.

Changes in a nation's food choices take time and have side effects which have to be considered. The working party has been realistic about time-scales. As well as long-term objectives, it has stated milestones to be achieved in the short-term (during the 1980s).

Q 17

Look at figure 1.2. Make a list of the people and organizations likely to be affected by a drop in consumer demand for sugar and foods which contain sugar.

The report recommends that education is the means by which these plans should be put into effect. This is clear from the title of the paper. The people doing the educating obviously include teachers in schools and colleges, but writers, broadcasters, advertisers, and medical advisers must also be involved. The working party is convinced that these educators should all speak with one voice. They should be given a clear message to put forward about nutrition and health.

Figure 15.12

The new diet must remain attractive and satisfying. During the Second World War, a very successful nutrition policy was adopted in Britain. .Rationing distributed food fairly among the population. The application of sound nutritional principles resulted in a better general standard of health than before or since the war.

Q 18
Why do you think that people did not stick to the war-time diet if it brought such good results?

Discuss in class the idea of nutritional goals and guidelines. Then try and answer the following questions.

Do you think a campaign based on nutritional guidelines would be successful?

Would it have your support?

What difficulties would it encounter?

How do you think the recommendations would affect the economy?

Which commercial interests might oppose it?

Ought the government to impose a healthy diet on the population with war-time style restrictions?

Are possible future changes likely to require different dietary guidelines?

CONCLUSION
The choice of food will always be an individual one. It is important that it is based on sound knowledge of nutrition.

BACKGROUND READING

FOOD STANDARDS
A little more than a hundred years ago there was no control of food quality whatsoever, and *adulteration* (diluting or disguising food with cheap ingredients) was widespread. Dishonest retailers had always engaged in adulteration, and this practice became much more widespread during the Industrial Revolution. The enormous scale of the problem in the early nineteenth century was revealed when a chemist, Fredrick Accum, began to investigate the problem scientifically and showed how dangerous the situation had become. His book, *A treatise on the adulteration of food and culinary poisons*, published in 1820, showed, for example, that pickles generally owed their appetizing green colour to copper salts; that highly coloured sweets were produced by adding very poisonous salts of copper and lead; and that most commercial bread was loaded with alum. He also found that Gloucester cheese was being given its orange colour with red lead, sand was being added to brown sugar, and milk was extensively watered.

Despite this scandalous state of affairs, little happened until 1850 when the medical journal *The Lancet* decided to take action and appointed two commissioners to investigate on their behalf. As a result of their investigations, Parliament passed the first Food and Drugs Act in 1860. This began to produce some control. In 1934 another review recommended that the law should be altered to ensure specific standards.

However, nothing changed until the Second World War, when the introduction of rationing meant that standards had to be prescribed for many different foods. This led eventually to the setting up of the Food Standards Committee in 1947. The Committee's job has been to advise the government about measures for preventing danger to health and loss of nutritive value, and generally protecting purchasers of food. In addition, a Food Additives and Contaminants Committee has been concerned with the special problem of the control of additives in food since 1954. In 1983, the two committees were combined to form the Food Advisory Committee.

The system which has been developed involves a great deal of discussion and consultation and has been widely copied in a number of other countries. It certainly provides protection from the bad practices which happened in the past and is generally and widely recognized to be an effective way of exerting control. For obvious reasons, food companies do everything they can to keep within the regulations, especially as the bad publicity in this area can seriously affect sales. In general, companies in the food industry welcome regulations, particularly for staple foods, because they prevent unfair competition and lay down the basic rules within which they can operate effectively.

Figure 15.13
High pressure liquid chromatography being used for food analysis at the Food Research Institute.

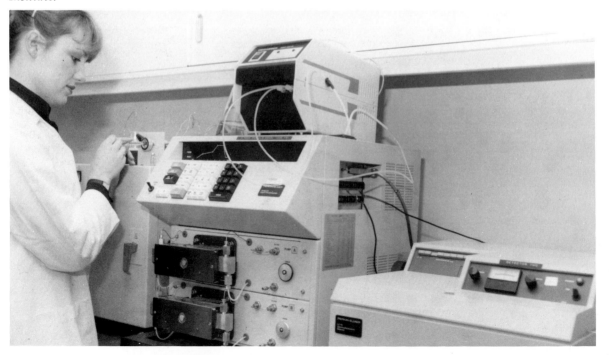

INDEX